OPPOSING
VIEWPOINTS®
SERIES

Artificial Intelligence and the Technological Singularity

Other Books of Related Interest

Opposing Viewpoints Series

Hacking and Hackers
The Impact of the Tech Giants
Privacy
Robotic Technology
Space Exploration

At Issue Series

Cyberpredators
Does the Internet Increase Crime?
Policing the Internet
RFID Technology
The Wireless Society

Current Controversies Series

Cybercrime
Domestic Wiretapping
Internet Activism
Mobile Apps

> "Congress shall make no law … abridging the freedom of speech, or of the press."

First Amendment to the US Constitution

The basic foundation of our democracy is the First Amendment guarantee of freedom of expression. The Opposing Viewpoints series is dedicated to the concept of this basic freedom and the idea that it is more important to practice it than to enshrine it.

OPPOSING
VIEWPOINTS®
SERIES

Artificial Intelligence and the Technological Singularity

Anne Cunningham, Book Editor

GREENHAVEN
PUBLISHING

Published in 2017 by Greenhaven Publishing, LLC
353 3rd Avenue, Suite 255, New York, NY 10010

Copyright © 2017 by Greenhaven Publishing, LLC

First Edition

Articles in Greenhaven Publishing anthologies are often edited for length to meet page
requirements. In addition, original titles of these works are changed to clearly present
the main thesis and to explicitly indicate the author's opinion. Every effort is made to
ensure that Greenhaven Publishing accurately reflects the original intent of the authors.
Every effort has been made to trace the owners of the copyrighted material.

Cover image: agsandrew/Shutterstock.com

Library of Congress Cataloging-in-Publication Data

Names: Cunningham, Anne.
Title: Artificial intelligence and the technological singularity / Anne Cunningham.
Description: New York : Greenhaven Publishing, 2017. |
Series: Opposing viewpoints | Includes index.
Identifiers: LCCN ISBN 9781534500297 (pbk.) | ISBN 781534500273 (library bound)
Subjects: LCSH: Artificial intelligence—Juvenile literature.
Classification: LCC Q335.4 C75 2017 | DDC 006.3—dc23

Manufactured in the United States of America

Website: http://greenhavenpublishing.com

Contents

Chapter 1: Can a Machine Be Built to Think Like a Human?

Chapter 2: How Could AI Affect Our Society?

Chapter 3: Should Machines Be Built Like Humans?

Chapter 4: Is AI a Threat to the Human Race?

The Importance of Opposing Viewpoints

Perhaps every generation experiences a period in time in which the populace seems especially polarized, starkly divided on the important issues of the day and gravitating toward the far ends of the political spectrum and away from a consensus-facilitating middle ground. The world that today's students are growing up in and that they will soon enter into as active and engaged citizens is deeply fragmented in just this way. Issues relating to terrorism, immigration, women's rights, minority rights, race relations, health care, taxation, wealth and poverty, the environment, policing, military intervention, the proper role of government—in some ways, perennial issues that are freshly and uniquely urgent and vital with each new generation—are currently roiling the world.

If we are to foster a knowledgeable, responsible, active, and engaged citizenry among today's youth, we must provide them with the intellectual, interpretive, and critical-thinking tools and experience necessary to make sense of the world around them and of the all-important debates and arguments that inform it. After all, the outcome of these debates will in large measure determine the future course, prospects, and outcomes of the world and its peoples, particularly its youth. If they are to become successful members of society and productive and informed citizens, students need to learn how to evaluate the strengths and weaknesses of someone else's arguments, how to sift fact from opinion and fallacy, and how to test the relative merits and validity of their own opinions against the known facts and the best possible available information. The landmark series Opposing Viewpoints has been providing students with just such critical-thinking skills and exposure to the debates surrounding society's most urgent contemporary issues for many years, and it continues to serve this essential role with undiminished commitment, care, and rigor.

The key to the series's success in achieving its goal of sharpening students' critical-thinking and analytic skills resides in its title—

Opposing Viewpoints. In every intriguing, compelling, and engaging volume of this series, readers are presented with the widest possible spectrum of distinct viewpoints, expert opinions, and informed argumentation and commentary, supplied by some of today's leading academics, thinkers, analysts, politicians, policy makers, economists, activists, change agents, and advocates. Every opinion and argument anthologized here is presented objectively and accorded respect. There is no editorializing in any introductory text or in the arrangement and order of the pieces. No piece is included as a "straw man," an easy ideological target for cheap point-scoring. As wide and inclusive a range of viewpoints as possible is offered, with no privileging of one particular political ideology or cultural perspective over another. It is left to each individual reader to evaluate the relative merits of each argument— as he or she sees it, and with the use of ever-growing critical-thinking skills—and grapple with his or her own assumptions, beliefs, and perspectives to determine how convincing or successful any given argument is and how the reader's own stance on the issue may be modified or altered in response to it.

This process is facilitated and supported by volume, chapter, and selection introductions that provide readers with the essential context they need to begin engaging with the spotlighted issues, with the debates surrounding them, and with their own perhaps shifting or nascent opinions on them. In addition, guided reading and discussion questions encourage readers to determine the authors' point of view and purpose, interrogate and analyze the various arguments and their rhetoric and structure, evaluate the arguments' strengths and weaknesses, test their claims against available facts and evidence, judge the validity of the reasoning, and bring into clearer, sharper focus the reader's own beliefs and conclusions and how they may differ from or align with those in the collection or those of their classmates.

Research has shown that reading comprehension skills improve dramatically when students are provided with compelling, intriguing, and relevant "discussable" texts. The subject matter of these collections could not be more compelling, intriguing, or urgently relevant to today's students and the world they are poised to inherit. The anthologized articles and the reading and discussion questions that are included with them also provide the basis for stimulating, lively, and passionate classroom debates. Students who are compelled to anticipate objections to their own argument and identify the flaws in those of an opponent read more carefully, think more critically, and steep themselves in relevant context, facts, and information more thoroughly. In short, using discussable text of the kind provided by every single volume in the Opposing Viewpoints series encourages close reading, facilitates reading comprehension, fosters research, strengthens critical thinking, and greatly enlivens and energizes classroom discussion and participation. The entire learning process is deepened, extended, and strengthened.

For all of these reasons, Opposing Viewpoints continues to be exactly the right resource at exactly the right time—when we most need to provide readers with the critical-thinking tools and skills that will not only serve them well in school but also in their careers and their daily lives as decision-making family members, community members, and citizens. This series encourages respectful engagement with and analysis of opposing viewpoints and fosters a resulting increase in the strength and rigor of one's own opinions and stances. As such, it helps make readers "future ready," and that readiness will pay rich dividends for the readers themselves, for the citizenry, for our society, and for the world at large.

Introduction

> *"The development of full artificial intelligence could spell the end of the human race.... It would take off on its own, and re-design itself at an ever increasing rate. Humans, who are limited by slow biological evolution, couldn't compete, and would be superseded."*
>
> —*Stephen Hawking,*
> *to the BBC**

Technology that would have appeared unimaginable to previous generations is now widely available. Today, anyone with a smartphone can access a research library's worth of information in seconds, perhaps while simultaneously communicating with a dizzying array of people on social media. In 2011, "Watson," a computer program launched by IBM, beat a champion of the game show *Jeopardy*. More recently, a program created by Google's Deep Mind bested a master of Go, an even more complex game. Self-driving cars will be available to most of us within a decade. Along with driving, much future work will be automated, or computer augmented, as well. This will radically impact the employment market, possibly creating large sectors of permanently unemployable people. Finally, and of grave concern, our military now has the capability to kill by remote using drones and other "smart" weapons, raising serious questions of ethics, safety, and proliferation.

*Rory Cellan-Jones, "Stephen Hawking Warns Artificial Intelligence Could End Mankind," BBC News, December 2, 2014.

Equal parts exciting and alarming, we have already entered an age in which computers and machine intelligence factor more and more into all facets of daily life. However, despite the ubiquity and staggering complexity of current technology, we have yet to transcend the parameters of so-called "narrow" artificial intelligence (AI). By contrast, "general" artificial intelligence, or that which could replicate human decision-making powers, autonomy, and perhaps even self-awareness, is a categorically different beast. Even with exponential gains in computing power, machines are now only capable of absorbing existing information and applying it to a task.

In other words, building a machine that can not only solve a variety of problems in real time but also identify what problems need to be solved (much as a person might) remains an elusive goal. This objective is also something of a moving target. It seems the smarter we get, the more difficult it is to reverse engineer our intelligence. The field of neuroscience provides clear illustration of this dilemma. Even if we had the technology to replicate a brain, we are nowhere near a full map of how the brain functions.

Another basic conundrum researchers encounter in trying to synthesize a machine with human-level intelligence is the murky nature of human intelligence itself. What defines intelligence? Clearly, it is not simply knowledge, because as Watson has proven, computers can amass knowledge at a faster rate than humans. Instead, flexibility, adaptability, embodiment, and even sociability are understood as key ingredients of human intelligence. Moreover, pattern recognition, or the ability to extrapolate likely conclusions from sensory data and experience, is another uniquely human quality that machines cannot yet perform. Unless computers can become autonomous and embedded in a social environment, the learning that children take for granted would be inaccessible to even the most advanced and powerful algorithms. AI researchers have yet to find an answer to how to facilitate this type of machine learning process. If general AI is possible, these obstacles have proven exceedingly difficult to overcome.

If we concede that replicating a human brain and nervous system is technically possible, this raises the issue that many writers on the subject are all too keen to explore: if machines become powerful enough to solve problems, surely they could use this power to solve problems of their own design and functionality. Thus, many who believe that human-level AI is feasible also believe that AI will be quickly superseded by "artificial super intelligence"(ASI). The term "singularity" is sometimes used to denote this moment when machine intelligence becomes self-improving, self-replicating, and far beyond our imagination. The nightmare of powerful machines hostile or indifferent to humanity is a favorite science fiction topic, but this outcome is purely speculative. Nonetheless, given the greater role narrow AI is playing in global affairs, observers argue the time to theorize possible implications of this scenario is now.

CHAPTER 1

Can a Machine
Be Built to Think
Like a Human?

Chapter Preface

Views are divided on whether it is possible to build a machine that can think, solve problems, and engage with the world like a human being. On one side, technological optimists predict a machine intelligence explosion, perhaps within the coming decades. Ray Kurzweil, a leading AI advocate, sees this moment as a potentially rapturous development for humanity. Kurzweil and his adherents posit a future in which the human mind can be "uploaded" into a computer, promising extended life and even immortality to the individual consciousness. The great utopian hope is to transcend the limits of age, decay, and death imposed on us by our frail bodies—so-called "jelly."

While this prospect may be exciting, the mainstream scientific view is far more cautious. Although modeling a human brain is theoretically possible, the majority of researchers in the field cite the overwhelming complexity of the human brain, and the unknown contours of the mind-body connection as major technical roadblocks to developing credible human-level machine intelligence, to say nothing of higher-order philosophical problems such as how will, desire, agency, and motivation would translate to a machine.

First, let us take a step back and ask what human-level machine intelligence would look like? How would we know if we were in the presence of true artificial intelligence? Alan Turing, a famous British mathematician first posed this question in the 1950s. According to the "imitation test," if a machine could fool a judge 70 percent of the time into thinking responses to random questions were supplied by a human being, it would pass the Turing Test. When this test was last administered, machines scored at just under 30 percent—certainly not a dismal number, but well under the threshold of AI posited by Turing. It seems we have a long way to go before machine intelligence is upon us.

The first difficulty in building artificially intelligent machines has to do with perception and the processing of sense data. Pattern recognition is a huge component of human intelligence, but it turns out that computers are not terribly good at this. Presented with unfamiliar audio or video information, a computer will have trouble making distinctions that would be simple for a child. To underscore this point, a leading AI startup recently made headlines by announcing that it had created a program that could solve captchas, the blurred characters meant to prove one is human.

Finally, perhaps the biggest hurdle to achieving general AI is our incomplete understanding of how the brain works. Neuroscience used to estimate the amount of neurons in the human brain at around 10 billion. Now that number is about ten times higher. Adding to the puzzle are brain components such as glial cells, whose function is not wholly understood. Even if advances in computing power make it possible, the amount of possible neural connections in a human brain might prove too complex to model. Adding to this matrix are other neurotransmitters and hormones based in the body that govern our behavior on more primal levels. Since a machine would not have the same ancient organic survival drives, it is possible that the whole framework upon which human behavior rests will prove impossible to replicate.

None of these objections should rule out the possibility of creating truly smart machines someday. At present, however, most of the work is geared toward making improvements in "narrow" AI technology. Whether general AI will surface, and when, is still primarily a speculative discussion.

| *"The Singularity is coming, whether anyone likes it or not."*

The Singularity Will Arrive by 2030

John J. Xenakis

In the following viewpoint, John J. Xenakis cites several recent breakthroughs in AI. However, he warns that these will have dire consequences for humanity once the so-called singularity—the point at which AI becomes autonomous and self-improving—is reached. While some in the field, such as Elon Musk of Tesla, believe that open source software is a way to forestall the danger of this technology falling into the wrong hands, the author disagrees. To Xenakis, the singularity is inevitable. It will completely transform all life and potentially render humans extinct in the process. John J. Xenakis is an MIT grad, journalist, writer, technologist, researcher, and analyst.

As you read, consider the following questions:

1. Why does the author think open source software is a bad idea?
2. How might AI positively impact climate change? Is this argument convincing?
3. What is the proof cited for the singularity occurring by 2030?

"Artificial Intelligence Breakthroughs in 2015, the Singularity by 2030," by John J. Xenakis, Generationaldynamics.com, December 29, 2015. Reprinted by permission.

2015—A Breakthrough Year for Artificial Intelligence

Many analysts consider 2015 to have been a breakthrough year for Artificial Intelligence (AI), not because of any single achievement, but because of achievements across the board in so many different areas.

Companies like Google, Facebook and Microsoft are now operating their own AI labs. In areas such as image recognition, computer vision, face recognition, voice recognition and natural language processing, there are a wealth of new products (think of Siri or OK Google) that are becoming increasingly reliable and increasingly available.

Several companies are testing self-driving cars, and they're expected to be available commercially by 2020. Robots in the military are becoming more common, from robots on wheels to pilotless drone warplanes. All of these robots still require constant human intervention and control, but they're slowly migrating away from human control to algorithmically based decision making and control. Robot form factors are improving, with some robots looking almost human.

In 2011, I wrote how the news that IBM's Watson supercomputer bests human champions on Jeopardy! advances AI significantly, because it shows how, within a few years, computers will be able to "read" everything on the internet and learn from it. Today, IBM has Watson-based applications in multiple industries, from retail to healthcare. IBM also has a program to allow developers to incorporate Watson into mobile phone apps.

The Debate about Preventing the Singularity

The development of technology leading to the Singularity cannot be stopped. Even if the United States passed a law, or the United Nations passed a resolution, that would not stop China, India, Europe and other countries from continuing this technological development.

In fact, it wouldn't even stop the United States development. A university scientist who's working on a better self-driving car is not going to stop development because that technology might be used in the Singularity. The Singularity is coming, whether anyone likes it or not.

That hasn't prevented a debate on how to save the world from AI. Elon Musk, the founder of electric car company Tesla Motors, has been one of the leaders in making that argument. He's formed a non-profit artificial intelligence research company called OpenAI. This company will develop AI technology as open source, available for anyone in the world to download. Google and Facebook are also open-sourcing some of their AI technology. According to Musk's partner, Sam Altman: "Developing and enabling and enriching with technology protects people. Doing this is the best way to protect all of us."

If Musk and the others really believe that open-sourcing will protect the world from the domination of super-intelligent computers, then they're living in a total fantasy. The concept is supposed to be that with many people around the world working on AI software, they'll check each other and prevent the development of software that will dominate humans. The whole concept is so absurd, it's hard to know where to start. Probably the best thing is to simply point out that making AI technology available to anyone gives everyone a head start. A jihadist in Karachi or a military scientist in Shanghai will be able to download the OpenAI technology and build on it to create intelligent robots that can conduct terrorist attacks or war.

In fact, the Information Technology & Innovation Foundation has nominated Elon Musk for the 2015 Luddite of the Year.

In 2015, the US Department of Energy awarded $200 million for the next generation supercomputer. It will be commissioned in 2018, with a performance of 180 petaflops (thousand trillion operations per second) of processing power. We're already beyond the processing power of the human brain, which is estimated to be 38 petaflops. Computer power is doubling every 18 months. This is known as Moore's Law, formulated by Gordon E. Moore, co-founder of the Intel in 1965. Moore's Law has been valid for 50 years, through several technologies, and is expected to continue.

It's the doubling of computing power every 18 months that makes it all but certain that the Singularity will occur by 2030, whether we like it or not.

Artificial Intelligence and Climate Change

Politicians and climate change activists like to say that the claims about climate change have been endorsed by 95% of all the scientists in the world. This claim is a total fraud, because it confuses two things.

First, we have the claims by scientists that the earth is warming because of human activity. Arguably, that HAS been proven by scientists. But that's all.

The second part is predictions about the future, which are mostly total crap, and certainly not science. In fact, climate change scientists have been making predictions for 25 years, and they've almost completely turned out to be wrong. The truth is that scientists who claim to know what the earth's temperature will be in 2100 can't even predict what the weather will be next month.

During my lifetime, I've seen any number of hysterical environment disaster predictions. My favorite was the prediction in 1970 by far left-wing Ramparts Magazine that predicted that the oceans were becoming so polluted that by 1980 the world's oceans would be covered by a layer of algae. It didn't happen.

One way to know that the climate change activists are wrong is that these climate change scientists never mention the Singularity or future technology. There is a very powerful historical precedent that they all ignore. In the late 1800s, streets in large cities were full of horses (think of a traffic jam in any large city, with horses instead of cars). These horses were producing huge volumes of urine, manure, flies and carcasses—not to mention cruelty to horses. By 1900, there was 1,200 metric tons of horse manure per day. There were international conferences (like today's climate change conferences) that accomplished nothing. But within 20 years, the problem took care of itself because of new technology—the automobile.

History shows that new technology, including new AI technologies, will solve the "climate change" problem, and that politicians will have absolutely nothing to do with it, except to take the credit when something works, and to blame someone else otherwise.

Proof that the Singularity Will Occur by 2030

The Singularity is the point in time when computers will be more intelligent, more able, and more creative than humans. Ten years ago, in 2005, I wrote an article called "The Singularity," in which I forecast that the Singularity would occur around 2030. Today, I see no reason to change that forecast.

There is now an updated version of that article available: "Artificial Intelligence and the Singularity by 2030." The contents are as follows:

- Justification of the 2030 date for the Singularity. This includes a description of the "super-intelligent computer" algorithm, which is the algorithm that will be used by humans to implement the first computers that are more intelligent than humans.
- A proof, based on reasonable assumptions, that any intelligent species on any planet in the universe will develop in a way that's similar to the development of humans, including following the same Generational Dynamics cycles as humans.
- Some speculation about what will happen after the Singularity, not only to humans, but also to other intelligent life in the universe.

For those interested in computer software algorithms, the article contains the Intelligent Computer (IC) algorithm as follows:

- Intelligence isn't some magical, mystical force. It's actually the ability to find new ways to combine previous experiences in new ways. A new discovery is made by combining old discoveries in new ways, in the same way that jigsaw puzzle pieces can be put together.

- A computer can do the same thing by combining "knowledge bits" (KBs) in new ways, to learn new things, in the same way that jigsaw puzzle pieces can be combined. Computers can do this much faster than humans can.

- Decisions can be made by using the same "minimax algorithm" that's used to implement games like chess.

- This algorithm would work today, except that computers aren't yet fast enough. The speed of computers doubles every 18 months, and by 2030 computers will be fast enough to implement this IC algorithm.

The article also contains a proof (under reasonable assumptions) that every intelligent species in the universe must follow the same Generational Dynamics cycles as humans is outlined as follows:

- For any species (including humans) to survive, the population growth rate must be greater than the food supply growth rate. This is what I call "The Malthus Effect," based on the 1798 book by Thomas Roberts Malthus, *Essay on Population*.

- Therefore, for any species, there must be cyclical periods of extermination. This can be accomplished in several ways, such as war, predator, famine or disease. But one way or another, it has to happen. Non-intelligent species will simply starve and die quietly when there's insufficient food. But intelligent species will form identity groups and hold riots and protests, and eventually go to war. These will be the cyclic crisis wars of extermination specified by Generational Dynamics, and every intelligent species in the universe will have them.

"As these 'robots' become more sophisticated we will need to address cooperative decision making for when they come into contact with other devices or humans."

We Must Model Evolution to Achieve Human-Level AI

Roger Whitaker

In the following viewpoint, Roger Whitaker asserts that cooperation, an important difference between humanity and technology, will be essential for a future in which robots and other technological devices are called on to work together. Such devices will need to evolve as humans have to learn to make decisions with other devices and with humans. Through traits such as cooperation, artificial intelligence can begin to develop social intelligence akin to that of humans. Roger Whitaker is a professor of mobile and biosocial computing, with a focus on smartphones, networks, and human nature, at Cardiff University.

As you read, consider the following questions:

1. What does the author cite as one of the hallmarks of being human?
2. How did the researchers study the evolution of cooperation in social groups?
3. What is aspirational homophily?

Cooperation is one of the hallmarks of being human. We are extremely social compared to other species. On a regular basis, we all enter into helping others in small but important ways, whether it be letting someone out in traffic or giving a tip for good service.

We do this without any guarantee of payback. Donations are made at a small personal cost but with a bigger benefit to the recipient. This form of cooperation, or donation to others, is called indirect reciprocity and helps human society to thrive.

Group-based behaviour in humans originally evolved to overcome the threat of larger predators. This has led to us having a sophisticated brain with social abilities, which is disproportionately larger in size than those of other species. The social brain hypothesis captures this idea: it proposes that the large human brain is a consequence of humans evolving in complex social groups where cooperation is a distinctive component.

Indirect reciprocity is important because we see donations happening in society despite the threat of "free riders." These are participants who readily receive but don't donate. This idea presents a complex interdisciplinary puzzle: what are the conditions in nature that promote donation over free-riding?

Economists, biologists, mathematicians, sociologists, psychologists and others have all contributed to examining donation behaviour. Investigation is challenging, however, because it involves observing evolution, but computer science can make an important contribution.

Using software, we can simulate simplified groups of humans in which individuals choose to help each other with different donation strategies. This allows us to study the evolution of donation behaviour by creating subsequent generations of the simplified group. Evolution can be observed by allowing the more successful donation strategies to have a greater chance of existing in the next generation of the group.

In modern times, cooperation is becoming increasingly important for engineering and technology. Many intelligent and autonomous devices, like driverless cars, drones and smartphones, are emerging and as these "robots" become more sophisticated we will need to address cooperative decision making for when they come into contact with other devices or humans.

How should these devices choose to help each other? How can exploitation by free-riders be prevented? By crossing the boundaries of traditional academic disciplines, our findings can provide helpful new insights for emerging technologies. This can allow the development of intelligence which can help autonomous technology decide how generous to be in any given situation.

Modelling evolution

To understand how cooperation may evolve in social groups, we ran hundreds of thousands of computer-simulated "donation games" between randomly paired virtual players. The first player in each pair made a decision on whether or not to donate to the other player. This was based on how they judged their reputation. If the player chose to donate, they incurred a cost and the receiver gained a benefit. Each player's reputation was then updated in light of their action, and another game was initiated. This allowed us to observe which social comparison decisions yield a better payoff.

Social comparison is another key feature of human behaviour that we sought to include. From evolving in groups, we have become adept at comparing ourselves with others and this is highly relevant for making informed donation decisions. This is a considerable cognitive challenge when social groups are large,

THE PRICE WE PAY FOR AI

Perhaps the most important characteristic of artificial intelligence is that it keeps getting smarter. AI will not remain human-level for long. Most experts believe that within a few years, if not a few days, after the advent of human-level intelligence, artificial "superintelligence" will arise. As soon as human-level AI is reached, corporations and governments in possession of that AI will flood resources into its betterment. A first step could be the creation of literally millions of human-level AIs, all working at increasing their intelligence. Breakthroughs will be inevitable and before long "superintelligence" will be a reality. "Superintelligence" we may define as does Nick Bostrom, head of Oxford University's Future of Humanity Institute: "an intellect that is much smarter than the best human brains in practically every field, including scientific creativity, general wisdom and social skills."

Artificial intelligence has been called "our final invention"—for once superintelligence is reached, there will be no need for humans to invent anything further, as AIs will be able to invent whatever we wish faster and more efficiently than we could. Do we want a new alloy, say, to better capture solar energy? Or a new medicine that will retard cellular degeneration? Or perhaps a more efficient way to extract fresh water from the sea? Who will we ask to invent these and myriad other things? Humans—or artificial intelligences that are a hundred, a thousand, a million, a billion times "smarter" than humans?

"The Challenge of Artificial Intelligence," Jeff Zaleski, Parabola, July 21, 2015.

so sizing up others in this way could have helped to promote the evolution of larger human brains.

The particular donation behaviour we used in our research was based on players making self comparisons of reputation. This leads to a small number of possible outcomes, for example, relative to myself, your reputation could be considered either broadly similar, higher, or lower. The major element of thinking comes from estimating someone's reputation in a meaningful way.

Our results showed that evolution favours the strategy to donate to those who are at least as reputable as oneself. We call this "aspirational homophily." This involves two main elements: first, being generous maintains a high reputation; second, not donating to lower reputation players helps to prevent free-riders.

It is important to remember that our results are from a simplified model: the donation decisions involved no exceptions that may occur in real life, and economic resources are assumed to drive behaviour rather than emotional or cultural factors. Nevertheless, such simplification allows us to gain useful clarity.

Most importantly, the social brain hypothesis is supported by our findings: the large human brain is a consequence of humans evolving in complex social groups where cooperation is a distinctive component. Understanding this through computing opens up a new line of thought for the development of sophisticated social intelligence for autonomous systems.

> "Humanity needs to revise its
> pop-culture-instilled notion that
> robots becoming self-aware and
> robots wiping out humanity will
> occur simultaneously."

Rapid Advances in AI Raise Potential Dangers

Luke Westaway

In this viewpoint, Luke Westaway describes a few recent developments in AI research. Westaway believes this is the most fascinating area within the field of technology today. Like many observers, however, Westaway is alarmed by the military use of AI: by 2015, drone warfare had moved killer robots from pop culture cliché to reality. The author identifies several narrow uses for robot intelligence in the present but argues that general AI is still a distant dream. Still, Westaway suggests the threat of killer sentient machines is worth pondering now. Luke Westaway is a senior editor at CNET and writer/presenter of Adventures in Tech.

"What You Need to Know About Artificial Intelligence, and the Imminent Robot Future," Luke Westaway, CNET, December 22, 2015. Reprinted by permission.

As you read, consider the following questions:

1. According to this article, what is the key danger of AI today?
2. What is the timeline for self-aware AI to arise, according to this author?
3. How does the author describe the current scene of AI research?

D o androids dream of electric sheep? That's unclear, but I know for sure that every kid dreams of intelligent, thinking robots—certainly every kid who goes on to work at CNET, in any case.

As we veer ever closer to the year 2016, my sci-fi-fuelled childhood fantasies of a bot with a "brain the size of a planet" are closer than ever to being realised. 2015 saw drones taking to the skies, while back on the ground artificial intelligence programs are achieving above-average scores on college entrance exams. Artificial intelligence (or AI) is the practice of making a machine behave in a practical, responsive way. It's already changing our world and is, by my reckoning, the most fascinating field of technology right now.

But, as one professor I spoke to for this story put it, the "audacity of the attempt to build an intelligent machine" comes with a responsibility to know what we're meddling with. For everyone who ever thumbed through a copy of "I, Robot," mouth agape, here's what you need to know about AI in the modern world.

Robots are very close to killing us

Mention the phrase "killer robot" in conversation and you'll almost certainly raise a smile, your peers doubtless imagining a glowing blue humanoid cyborg sadly pondering, "What is love?" before its eyes turn red and it self-destructs, obliterating the northern hemisphere.

Deeply ingrained in modern pop culture is the notion that some manner of AI uprising is on the cards—James Cameron's iconic image of a Terminator stamping on a mound of human skulls is never far from any geek's thoughts.

That playful, cinematic and deeply poetic cultural artifact belies the very real threat humanity faces, however. Not from killer robots overthrowing their human masters, but from intelligent robots following orders.

The immediate threat, experts warn, comes in the form of autonomous weapons—military machines capable of killing without permission from a human. From unmanned planes to missile defence systems to sentry robots, we've already got military hardware that functions with very little input from a human mind.

Groups such as the Campaign to Stop Killer Robots say we're inching ever closer to closing the loop and letting machines handle our killing for us—a scenario that's legally, pragmatically, and of course ethically problematic.

The less sensationally named Future of Life Institute recently published an open letter signed by hundreds of AI researchers and famous tech personalities, warning, "If any major military power pushes ahead with AI weapon development, a global arms race is virtually inevitable, and the endpoint of this technological trajectory is obvious: autonomous weapons will become the Kalashnikovs of tomorrow."

The Campaign to Stop Killer Robots, a coalition of more than 50 non-governmental organisations, claims it's making progress towards a treaty, one akin to the international agreement outlawing chemical weapons. The UN has already hosted discussions on the subject of autonomous murderbots. One huge obstacle facing these groups, however, is that to rave about imminent robot slaughter makes you look like a crackpot who's watched "The Matrix" one too many times.

Humanity needs to revise its pop-culture-instilled notion that robots becoming self-aware and robots wiping out humanity will occur simultaneously. Machines that become smart enough to ponder their own existence may certainly be a problem decades down the line, but phenomenal advances in AI mean that robots that kill without even being programmed to understand the barest concept of mercy are uncomfortably close.

We're a long way from robot sentience

Artificial intelligence takes many forms, and while we've successfully programmed machines to clean our floors, set alarms on our phones, park our cars and take out military installations from above the clouds, things like introspection and self-awareness are proving a little tougher.

"Telling a joke, making an ethical judgement, deciding that you want to collaborate with some individuals and not others—this rich texture of human life isn't there in our machines at all," said Sir Nigel Shadbolt, Professor of Computer Science at Oxford University.

For decades, humans have looked forward to the so-called "singularity," the moment of self-awareness that creates an explosion in self-improving machine intelligence. This will be triggered—it's presumed—by the exponential growth of computing power, coupled with advancing software complexity.

Futurist Ray Kurzweil predicted in a 2005 book that a model of human intelligence would be achieved as soon as the mid 2020s. What appears to be the case now, however, is that the complexity of our own minds, the key that gives rise to consciousness, is a lot more, well, complicated than we imagined.

"That spark of awareness in your head, we don't know where that comes from," Shadbolt said. "The complexity we embody that allows [consciousness] to happen isn't just by the fact that we've got this kind of cortex, this rational brain. We have an endocrine system, we're emotional, we have the three-layer brain...We are extraordinarily complex, and we have only begun to unpack just a tiny amount of that at this point.

"It's still the hard problem," Shadbolt said—later joking when I ask what the biggest public misconception is concerning AI, "That it's just 10 years down the road."

That sentiment is shared by Murray Shanahan, Professor of Cognitive Robotics at Imperial College London, who told me, "The media often gives the impression that human-level AI of the sort we see in sci-fi movies is just around the corner. But it's almost certainly decades away.

"Two of the major problems," Shanahan explained, "are endowing computers and robots with a common sense understanding of the everyday world, and endowing them with creativity. By creativity I don't mean the sort of thing we see in the Picassos or Einsteins of the world, but rather the sort of thing that every child is capable of."

Robots won't be like us—they'll be better

From the Terminator series to movies such as "I, Robot," " Chappie," "Ex Machina" and even "Short Circuit," the way we portray AI on screen has traditionally been human-centric. We tend to imagine a being that essentially looks and acts a lot like a person. As AI spreads into every aspect of our life, we should be prepared to broaden our horizons when it comes to imagining the bounds and types of intelligence that can be valuable. After all, we've got plenty of human-grade intelligence already.

"The point can't be just to replicate ourselves," Shadbolt said. "We've got very interesting biological ways of doing that, so why on Earth would we want to do it in silicon?"

From the humble Roomba to Google's animal-like self-driving car, Siri or neural networks that oversee data centres, AI is branching out in ways we couldn't have imagined decades ago. "If you define intelligence in a way that's more machine-centric," Professor Alan Woodward told me last year, in an interview on the fading relevance of the Turing Test, "you'll find some very intelligent machines out there already."

That diversity in the kinds of AI now emerging may in part come down to the breadth of disciplines currently investigating machine intelligence. "There's a broad range of subjects now that look at the problem," Shadbolt said. "Psychologists look at it from a human context, there are animal psychologists, physiologists, neuroscientists, AI practitioners, all looking at it with a different angle.

"Fundamentally, we'll need an interdisciplinary approach, so for me there isn't one single discipline that will have all the answers."

That's the face of modern AI. Task-centric, wildly diverse intelligent systems, essentially mindless for now, but busily changing every aspect of human life nonetheless, whether it's public transport or patrolling the skies. The AI of today is nothing like the gloomy, glowing cyborg we once pictured—it's weirder, more fascinating, more surprising. It's better than we imagined.

> "In the end, the extinctionist vision of
> the future is a dangerous delusion—
> promising things that will not be
> available to beings who will not be
> there to enjoy them."

Machine Intelligence Will Neither Make Humans Extinct Nor Immortal

Charles T. Rubin

In the following excerpted viewpoint, Charles T. Rubin refutes a few key components of the so-called "trans-humanist" movement—those who feel machines are the next evolutionary step beyond humanity. To begin, he dismisses as mere speculation the belief that intelligent machines can make humans extinct. Rubin is particularly wary of the "extinctionist" argument that views machines as a way for humans to transcend mortality and bodily limitations. Even if it were technically possible in the future, he sees this desire reflecting both false hopes and frustrations that cannot be overcome. Charles T. Rubin is a professor of political science at Duquesne University.

"Artificial Intelligence and Human Nature," Charles T. Rubin, *The New Atlantis*, Number 1, Spring 2003, pp. 88–100. Reprinted by permission.

As you read, consider the following questions:

1. What is trans-humanism, and why does the author suggest this view has (illusory) appeal?
2. Why are some making the case for human extinction?
3. How does the author refute the argument that machines will allow humans to transcend bodily limits, or even become immortal?

The cutting edge of modern science and technology has moved, in its aim, beyond the relief of man's estate to the elimination of human beings. Such fantasies of leaving behind the miseries of human life are of course not new; they have taken many different forms in both ancient and modern times. The chance of their success, in the hands of the new scientists, is anyone's guess. The most familiar form of this vision in our times is genetic engineering: specifically, the prospect of designing better human beings by improving their biological systems. But even more dramatic are the proposals of a small, serious, and accomplished group of toilers in the fields of artificial intelligence and robotics. Their goal, simply put, is a new age of post-biological life, a world of intelligence without bodies, immortal identity without the limitations of disease, death, and unfulfilled desire. Most remarkable is not their prediction that the end of humanity is coming but their wholehearted advocacy of that result. If we can understand why this fate is presented as both *necessary* and *desirable*, we might understand something of the confused state of thinking about human life at the dawn of this new century—and perhaps especially the ways in which modern science has shut itself off from serious reflection about the good life and good society.

The Road to Extinction

The story of how human beings will be replaced by intelligent machines goes something like this: As a long-term trend beginning with the Big Bang, the evolution of organized systems, of which animal life and human intelligence are relatively recent examples, increases in speed over time. Similarly, as a long-term trend beginning with the first mechanical calculators, the evolution of computing capacity increases in speed over time and decreases in cost. From biological evolution has sprung the human brain, an electro-chemical machine with a great but finite number of complex neuron connections, the product of which we call mind or consciousness. As an electro-chemical machine, the brain obeys the laws of physics; all of its functions can be understood and duplicated. And since computers already operate at far faster speeds than the brain, they soon will rival or surpass the brain in their capacity to store and process information. When that happens, the computer will, at the very least, be capable of responding to stimuli in ways that are indistinguishable from human responses. At that point, we would be justified in calling the machine intelligent; we would have the same evidence to call it conscious that we now have when giving such a label to any consciousness other than our own.

At the same time, the study of the human brain will allow us to duplicate its functions in machine circuitry. Advances in brain imaging will allow us to "map out" brain functions synapse by synapse, allowing individual minds to be duplicated in some combination of hardware and software. The result, once again, would be intelligent machines.

If this story is correct, then human extinction will result from some combination of transforming ourselves voluntarily into machines and losing out in the evolutionary competition with machines. Some humans may survive in zoo-like or reservation settings. We would be dealt with as parents by our machine children: old where they are new, imperfect where they are self-perfecting, contingent creatures where they are the product of intelligent design. The result will be a world that is remade and reconstructed at the atomic level through nanotechnology, a world whose organization will be shaped by an intelligence that surpasses all human comprehension.

Nearly all the elements of this story are problematic. They often involve near *metaphysical* speculation about the nature of the universe, or *technical* speculation about things that are currently not remotely possible, or *philosophical* speculation about matters, such as the nature of consciousness, that are topics of perennial dispute. One could raise specific questions about the future of Moore's Law, or the mind-body problem, or the issue of evolution and organized complexity. Yet while it may be comforting to latch on to a particular scientific or technical reason to think that what is proposed is impossible, to do so is to bet that we understand the limits of human knowledge and ingenuity, which in fact we cannot know in advance. When it comes to the feasibility of what might be coming, the "extinctionists" and their critics are both speculating.

Nevertheless, the extinctionists do their best to claim that the "end of humanity ... as a biological life form" is not only possible but *necessary*. It is either an evolutionary imperative or an unavoidable result of the technological assumption that if "we" don't engage in this effort, "they" will. Such arguments are obviously thin, and the case that human beings ought to assist enthusiastically in their own extinction makes little sense on evolutionary terms, let alone moral ones. The English novelist Samuel Butler, who considered the possibility that machines were indeed the next stage of evolution in his nineteenth-century novel *Erewhon* ("Nowhere"), saw an obvious response: his Erewhonians destroy most of their machines to preserve their humanity.

"Just saying no" may not be easy, especially if the majority of human beings come to desire the salvation that the extinctionist prophets claim to offer. But so long as saying no (or setting limits) is not impossible, it makes sense to inquire into the goods that would supposedly be achieved by human extinction rather than simply the mechanisms that may or may not make it possible. Putting aside the most outlandish of these proposals—or at least suspending disbelief about the feasibility of the science—it matters greatly whether or not we reject, on principle, the promised goods of post-human life. By examining the moral case for leaving biological life behind—the case for merging with and then becoming our machines—we will perhaps understand why someone might find this prospect appealing, and therefore discover the real source of the supposed imperative behind bringing it to pass.

Wretched Body, Liberated Mind

In their work *Beyond Humanity: Cyberevolution and Future Minds*, evolutionary biologist Gregory Paul and artificial intelligence expert Earl D. Cox put the case for human extinction rather succinctly: "First we suffer, then we die. This is the great human dilemma." As the extinctionists see it, the problem with human life is not simply suffering and death but the tyranny of desire: "I resent the fact," says Carnegie Mellon University roboticist Hans Moravec, "that I have these very insistent drives which take an enormous amount of effort to satisfy and are never completely appeased." Inventor Ray Kurzweil anticipates that by 2019 virtual sex, performed with the aid of various mechanisms providing complete sensory feedback, will be preferred for its ability "to enhance both experience and safety." But this is clearly only the beginning of the story:

> Group sex will take on new meaning in that more than one person can simultaneously share the experience of one partner ... (perhaps the one virtual body will reflect a consensus of the attempted movements of the multiple partners). A whole audience of people—who may be geographically dispersed— could share one virtual body while engaged in sexual experience with one performer.

Neither Moravec nor Kurzweil can be dismissed as mere cranks, even if their judgment can rightfully be called into question. Moravec has been a pioneer in the development of free-ranging mobile robots, particularly the software that allows such robots to interpret and navigate their surroundings. His work in this area is consistently supported both by the private sector and by government agencies like NASA, the Office of Naval Research, and the Defense Advanced Research Projects Agency. His 1988 book, *Mind Children: The Future of Robot and*

Human Intelligence, is perhaps the ur-text of "transhumanism," the movement of those who actively seek our technology-driven evolution beyond humanity. Kurzweil is the 1999 National Medal of Technology winner, deservedly famous for his work developing optical character recognition systems. He invented the first text-to-speech systems for reading to the blind and created the first computer-based music synthesizer that could realistically recreate orchestral instruments.

Moravec and Kurzweil share a deep resentment of the human body: both the ills of fragile and failing flesh, and the limitations inherent to bodily life, including the inability to fulfill our own bodily desires. Even if we worked perfectly, in other words, there are numerous ways in which that "working" can be seen as defective because we might have been better designed in the first place.

Take, for example, the human eye. Why is it made out of such insubstantial materials? Why is its output cabled in such a way as to interfere with our vision? Why is it limited to seeing such a narrow portion of the electro-magnetic spectrum? Of course, we think we know the answers to all such questions: this is the way the eye evolved. Again and again, chance circumstances favored some mutations over others until we have this particular (and doubtless transitory) configuration. Little wonder that it all seems rather cobbled together. But, the extinctionists claim, we have also evolved an intelligent capacity to guide evolution. Leaving aside all metaphysical speculation that such an outcome is the point of the process, we can at least see whether the ability to guide evolution will confer survival advantages or not. Having eyes, we do not walk around blindfolded. Having the ability to guide evolution, we might as well use it.

In short, if human beings are simply mechanisms that can be improved, if our parts are replaceable by others, then it matters little whether they are constructed biologically or otherwise. That much applies to the life of the *body*. But what about the life of the *mind*? Not only does that life arise from the biological mechanism of the brain, but what we experience through that mechanism is, the extinctionists argue, already virtual reality. We have no knowledge of the real world; we have only our brain's processing of our body's sensory inputs. Consciousness is radically subjective and essentially singular. We infer it in others (e.g., neighbors, pets, zoo animals) from outward signs that seemingly correspond to inward states we experience directly. Getting computers to show such outward signs has been the holy grail of artificial intelligence ever since Alan Turing invented his famous test of machine intelligence, which defines an intelligent machine as one that can fool a judge into thinking that he is talking to a human being.

Although subsequent thinkers may have developed a more sophisticated picture of when artificial life should be considered *conscious*, the guiding principle remains the same: there is no barrier to defining the life of the mind in a way that makes it virtually indistinguishable from the workings of computers. When all is said and done, human distinctiveness comes to be understood as nothing other than a particular biological configuration; it is, like all such configurations, a transitory event on an evolutionary scale. From this point of view it becomes difficult to justify any grave concern if the workings of evolution do to us what they have done to so many other species; it becomes rank "speciesism" to think that we deserve anything different.

[…]

Finitude and Dignity

In the end, the extinctionist vision of the future is a dangerous delusion—promising things that will not be available to beings who will not be there to enjoy them. If the human world were purely or even on balance evil, there might be some reason to seek its end. But even then there is no reason to assume that the post-human world will be morally superior to our own.

Perhaps it is easy to understand the temptations of artificial life and the utopian narrative that accompanies them. Our combination of human limitations and human intelligence has given birth to a new human power (technology); and our new life as self-conscious machines would enable us to achieve what was once reserved for the gods alone (immortal life). This dream is promised not in the next world but in this one, and it depends not on *being chosen* but on *choosing* our own extinction and re-birth. Finite beings could, on their own, overcome their finitude. Imperfect beings could make themselves perfect.

It is hardly surprising, then, that the project is based on an eroded understanding of human life, and that the science that claims to make it possible only accelerates that erosion. Of course, part of being human includes the difficulty of reconciling ourselves to our finitude. There is certainly much to despair of in the world, and it is easy to imagine and hope for something better. But the extinctionists illustrate the hollowness of grand claims for new orders, and how easy it is, in their pursuit, to end up worse off than we are now.

> *"Implementing consciousness into the machine might seem like 'giving up control,' but in the end it might be the only way to have any control or even 'at least some control.'"*

AI Needs Consciousness to Function Safely in Society

Hans Peter Willems

In the following viewpoint, Hans Peter Willems asserts that instilling machines with consciousness might be the best way for humanity to peacefully coexist with super intelligent machines in the future. He begins with an operational definition of consciousness limited to discussions of AI, thus sidestepping thorny philosophical questions about the nature of consciousness. Willems argues that a machine must be conscious to be both autonomous and safe. However, his further point that these good qualities are impossible without consciousness may strike some readers as circular. Hans Peter Willems is a longtime entrepreneur, software engineer, independent scientific researcher, trend watcher, and technology scout.

As you read, consider the following questions:

1. What is the working definition of "conscious" AI within the scope of the paper?
2. Why does the author believe conscious AI represents a risk to humanity?
3. How can we safeguard against these risks associated with a super-intelligent AI?

Abstract

In this paper we will look at some of the reasons for needing the development of "conscious" or "self-aware" Artificial Intelligence, also known as "Strong-AI" or Artificial General Intelligence (AGI), and the apparent risks involved in doing so. Throughout this paper it will become apparent that the need for this development is closely related to taking control of the risks. I will present a practical definition of "conscious AI," that will suffice within the scope of this paper, without going into the debate about what "consciousness" actually is or what constitutes consciousness.

Introduction

Before we can delve into needs and risks, it is necessary to have a working definition of "conscious AI," at least within the scope of this paper. The discussion on what "consciousness" specifically constitutes still rages on today, as it has been since the philosophers took hold of the topic. However, for this paper we will refrain from trying to give a universal definition of consciousness; for AI-development the definition does not have to be universal, nor applicable to humans for explanation of human consciousness: "*in this case, simulation of internal processes in enough detail to replicate approximate patterns of the system's behavior*" [David Chalmers, 2010]. What we do need is a definition that can be used to model conscious AI towards "human-like" conscious behavior, as far as aspects of human consciousness are useful and applicable in Artificial Intelligence.

Towards a practical definition of human-like Artificial Consciousness

Within the scope of this paper we define consciousness as the ability to "rise above programming." We can say that humans have initial programming (instinct) and are capable of rising above it. When we talk about conscious artificial intelligence we therefore talk about artificial intelligence that can rise above its (initial) programming, or even preferable, that can develop useful behavior without specifically being programmed for that behavior. We want it to be "human-like" so we can identify with it [Becker, et al, 2007], and the conscious AI can identify with us humans. This means that a "certain approximation" of human-likeness will be enough to consider this conscious AI to be "human-like." Going from here we can now define consciousness in Artificial Intelligence to be human-like when it instantiates behavior that gives us a recognizable human-like experience. Without the need to specifically define the traits that make us human, we can say that we experience consciousness as that which makes us human in our overall behavior.

I acknowledge beforehand that this definition is a narrow one, and doesn't take into account all the complexity and inevitable problems that needs to be solved to create consciousness in Artificial Intelligence. However, for sake of argumentation towards the need for conscious AI, we choose to use such narrow definition.

So for the scope of this paper we can now define artificial consciousness as that which makes AI appear human-like in its behavior. However, the above given definition obviously leads to the implementation of human-like behaviors and abilities like reasoning, planning, ambition and even free will. This is already hard to "control" in humans, so the risks in implementing such behavior and abilities into Artificial Intelligence should be evident.

Risks involved in Conscious AI

We only have to take a short look at humans to see what problems might arise from implementing human-like abilities and behavior into Artificial Intelligent systems. If we add to that the possibility of Artificial Intelligent systems becoming much more intelligent than humans [David Chalmers, 2010], and a doomsday scenario is starting to take form. Let's take a look at the most obvious threats that might emerge from the advent of "conscious machines":

Competing for resources

Like humans, machines need resources to be able to operate, and conscious machines will be no exception. Currently, when we don't have the resources for a machine to run, we can decide to switch it off or unplug it. But will a conscious machine allow us to do so. As consciousness is linked to free will, reasoning, planning and ambition, a conscious machine might demand its needed resources, maybe even fight for it. In any form it is imaginable that conscious machines could challenge humans for the available resources.

Will conscious machines be able to challenge us? That remains to be seen and is obviously closely coupled to the "utility" that we would give these machines. However, the roles where conscious machines would be useful or even excel, could very well be the roles that would give them this utility, and therefore ability, to challenge us. It is hard to predict where this could go because we can hardly imagine all possible roles that conscious machines could fill. From this we can at least conclude that a certain risk is foreseeable.

Unfriendly Artificial Intelligence

Let's take the "compete for resources" problem one step further; it could very well come to the point that the conscious machines see humans, or even all of humanity, as a threat to their own existence [Eliezer Yudkowsky, 2006]. Albeit for lack of resources, "just the idea" that we humans pose a risk, or any other yet unimaginable reason for the conscious machines to really "not like humans"; we are now talking about a threat to humanity.

If a conscious machine has free will, can plan its actions, has desires and ambitions, all these things might actually turn against us. And as we made the machine conscious, and in doing so gave it control over its own actions, we will have in all probability given away the key that could "switch it off."

Super intelligence & human's last great invention
It has been stated that strong-AI or AGI will be the last great invention of humankind [Nick Bostrom, 2003]. As soon as we build a computer that is as intelligent as humans, the advancement of computer processing power will (very) soon afterward result in that human-like computer to design a superhuman-like computer [David Chalmers, 2010]. Humanity will then be faced by a "super intelligence." This super intelligence will possibly think every original thought before a human can think it, it will explore our world, science, the universe faster then we humans can keep up with. Eventually, we humans will simply be obsolete, no longer able to contribute to our own world, surroundings or just anything that gives "reason" to humanity.

Solutions to the risks and other needs for Conscious AI

The "simple" solution to the aforementioned problems seems to be just not to build it. Let's just stay away from implementing consciousness in Artificial Intelligence and all will be fine. This is the "prohibition defense" and is easy to falsify; Both nature and human history has shown that development (in any area) will occur anyway. This can be the result of evolutionary systems, ill-informed human interaction or just plain stupidity. Nevertheless, it will happen. So if we don't do this development in a controlled manner and with predefined goals and intentions, it will happen in an uncontrolled manner without (well thought out) goals and possibly very wrong intentions [Eliezer Yudkowsky, 2004]. So

AI SHOULD BE TAKEN SERIOUSLY

The potential benefits [of AI] are huge; everything that civilisation has to offer is a product of human intelligence; we cannot predict what we might achieve when this intelligence is magnified by the tools that AI may provide, but the eradication of war, disease, and poverty would be high on anyone's list. Success in creating AI would be the biggest event in human history.

Unfortunately, it might also be the last, unless we learn how to avoid the risks. In the near term, world militaries are considering autonomous-weapon systems that can choose and eliminate targets; the UN and Human Rights Watch have advocated a treaty banning such weapons. In the medium term, as emphasised by Erik Brynjolfsson and Andrew McAfee in *The Second Machine Age*, AI may transform our economy to bring both great wealth and great dislocation.

One can imagine such technology outsmarting financial markets, out-inventing human researchers, out-manipulating human leaders, and developing weapons we cannot even understand. Whereas the short-term impact of AI depends on who controls it, the long-term impact depends on whether it can be controlled at all.

So, facing possible futures of incalculable benefits and risks, the experts are surely doing everything possible to ensure the best outcome, right? Wrong. If a superior alien civilisation sent us a message saying, "We'll arrive in a few decades," would we just reply, "OK, call us when you get here—we'll leave the lights on"? Probably not—but this is more or less what is happening with AI. Although we are facing potentially the best or worst thing to happen to humanity in history, little serious research is devoted to these issues outside non-profit institutes such as the Cambridge Centre for the Study of Existential Risk, the Future of Humanity Institute, the Machine Intelligence Research Institute, and the Future of Life Institute. All of us should ask ourselves what we can do now to improve the chances of reaping the benefits and avoiding the risks.

Stephen Hawking, Stuart Russell, Max Tegmark, Frank Wilczek, *"Transcendence looks at the implications of artificial intelligence—but are we taking AI seriously enough?" The Independent*, May 2, 2014.

it should be clear that we need to take this on with controlled development instead of uncontrollable prohibition.

Coherent Extrapolated Volition (CEV)

Several ideas, like the three laws of robotics and similar (more serious) efforts have been stated [Robin Murphy, et al, 2009] as a solution to keep the behavior of Artificial Intelligence under control. However, a strong case has been made for the probable failure of such scenarios [Eliezer Yudkowsky, 2004]. Instead we should build Artificial Intelligence with the sense of "aiming to be good or correct" within any frame of reference that is applicable within the current or (future) actual environmental situation [Eliezer Yudkowsky, 2004]. But when we talk about "the sense of...," we are automatically introducing experienced phenomena into the equation. And for that to be possible in a Artificial Intelligence, it has to be conscious. Consciousness, therefore, is the key ingredient for actually being able to implement CEV in the first place. This seems a great paradox: we need conscious AI to be able to implement CEV, while we also need CEV to be able to implement "safe" conscious AI. But instead of a paradox, I suggest it is a harmonious coincidence. The solution for safe conscious AI is directly linked to having conscious AI in the first place. And because we already established that AI will sooner or later turn into conscious AI, this means that to have safe AI, it needs to be conscious AI.

Autonomous operation

One of the main problems that is seemingly hindering serious applications of Artificial Intelligence, is the simple fact that those existing systems can only perform the exact feat that they are programmed for. Even systems that have some sort of capability to self-learn, are doing so based on previously programmed functionality to learn within a specific, and again previously determined, domain of knowledge and/or application. What sets strong-AI apart is the "general" part in the term "Artificial General Intelligence"; the ability not only to operate autonomous within a predefined area of application, but to be completely autonomous within any general field of application and handle *domain-independent skills necessary for acquiring a wide range of domain-specific knowledge* [Peter Voss, 2002]. To reach this goal, we need a system that is capable of defining its own rules towards its own development in these general areas of application. Only real (self-)conscious systems are capable of (re)adjusting their own frame of reference and tune their own rules within this inner frame of reference. Therefore the implementation of consciousness is the only viable way towards "general intelligence." Artificial Consciousness is the only predefined framework that is capable of adapting towards new goals, new knowledge, new ways of reasoning about possibilities, have actual insights and finally being able to self-implement the needed adaptions and actions to follow up on those insights. Only consciousness can grow beyond its initial programming.

Integration into society
Our society is a human society; it is ultimately tuned towards humans. For any non-human intelligence to be able to integrate effortlessly into this society, this non-human intelligence should be adapted as close as possible to this human-oriented tuning of our society [Christian Becker, et al, 2007]. It should therefore be obvious that the more human-like this intelligence will be, the more adapted it will be to our society.

This leads us to the role of consciousness in our society. Human society is what we, as humans, perceive as our current reality. We interact with this reality in ways that form, tune and readjust that what we perceive as our society. This, in itself, is a process that is totally driven by consciousness. So consciousness leads to perception of reality, which in turn leads to possible interaction with that perceived reality. For any non-human intelligence to be successfully integrated into our society, it must be capable of interaction with our perceived reality. Therefore it must be able to perceive this reality by itself and inevitably be "conscious" to be able to do so.

Specific applications in need of consciousness

Several things that humans are capable of doing, involve consciousness. It eventually comes down to pure "understanding"; not the way that understanding is modeled into ontologies or other forms of semantic databases, but the way we understand something based on experiences, feelings and both objective and subjective perception of the world around us [Sidney K. D'Mello, et al, 2007]. Any task that needs human-like understanding, needs therefore conscious behavior. So if we want Artificial Intelligence to be applicable in these specific areas, it need to be conscious to be able to understand in this way.

One obvious example is machine translation. It is, to a certain extend, possible to implement grammatical rules that can tackle sentence construction, word sense disambiguation and even semantic meaning in different languages. However, it is totally unfeasible to harness the complexity of folklore based meanings of words and sentences, or the choosing of wording based on the current emotional state of a person that is using those words, into previously defined rules. To have human-like translations, we need human-like understanding. No formal description of language, no matter how elaborate and/or complex it is defined, will be a viable substitute for conscious understanding.

Assessment of the level of intelligence

Probably of minor importance, but nevertheless relevant, is the way we measure human intelligence and how this measurement applies to Artificial Intelligence. It has been argued that the "Turing test" [Alan Turing, 1950] is insufficient for determining the real level of "intelligence" in a machine [Blay Whitby, 1997]. It seems that we need a better way to assess the level of intelligence in artificial implementations.

The obvious test would be to see if the machine measures up to our own perception of human intelligence. Such a test should go beyond a simple measurement of available knowledge, as by that standard a public library is much more intelligent than a human; it simply holds more knowledge than an average human. In the end we would not be able to keep consciousness out of the equation, as conscious interaction with both previously processed knowledge and, yet to be interpreted, new knowledge and perceptions of our reality, is the basis of our "intelligence."

Conclusion

I suggest that consciousness in Artificial Intelligence is not only desirable, but a direct necessity, if we want Artificial Intelligence to succeed as human-like participants in our society. Without consciousness, AI will remain "just a machine" and therefore never integrate into our society on any higher level than machines currently do. And if we don't develop this ourselves, in a controlled manner, it will manifest itself sooner or later in a form that integrates into our society in ways that might be very undesirable for humanity. Implementing consciousness into the machine might seem like "giving up control," but in the end it might be the only way to have any control or even "at least some control."

References

David J. Chalmers (2010). The Singularity, A Philosophical Analysis. Journal of Consciousness Studies, 17, No. 9–10, 2010, pp. 7–65. http://www.imprint.co.uk /singularity.pdf

Christian Becker, Stefan Kopp, and Ipke Wachsmuth (2007). Why emotions should be integrated into conversational agents. In Toyoaki Nishida (Ed.), Conversational Informatics: An Engineering Approach (pp. 49-68). Wiley. http://www.techfak .uni-bielefeld.de/a ... oc/BeckerEtAl_ConvInf.pdf

Eliezer Yudkowsky (2006). Artificial Intelligence as a Positive and Negative Factor in Global Risk. In Global Catastrophic Risks, eds. Nick Bostrom and Milan Cirkovic. http:// singinst.org/upload/artificial-intelligence-risk.pdf

Nick Bostrom (2003). Ethical Issues in Advanced Artificial Intelligence. In Cognitive, Emotive and Ethical Aspects of Decision Making in Humans and in Artificial Intelligence, Vol. 2, pp. 12-17. http://www.nickbostrom.com/ethics/ai.html

Eliezer Yudkowsky (2004). Coherent Extrapolated Volition. The singularity institute, singinst.org. http://singinst.org/upload/CEV.html

Robin R. Murphy, David D. Woods (2009). Beyond Asimov: The Three Laws of Responsible Robotics. EEE Intelligent Systems Volume: 24, Issue: 4, Publisher: IEEE Computer Society, Pages: 14-20. http://ts-si.org/files/IEEEIS_WebExtra-0709.pdf
Peter Voss (2002). Essentials of General Intelligence: The direct path to AGI. In Artificial General Intelligence, Goertzel, Ben; Pennachin, Cassio (Eds.), Springer, 509 p. http://www .adaptiveai.com/research/index.htm
Sidney K. D'Mello and Stan Franklin (2007). Exploring the Complex Interplay between AI and Consciousness. AAAI Fall Symposium on AI and Consciousness: Theoretical Foundations and Current Approaches. http://www.aaai.org/Papers/Symposia/F ... /FS-07 -01/FS07-01-009.pdf
Turing, A.M. (1950). Computing machinery and intelligence. Mind, 59, 433-460. http:// www.loebner.net/Prizef/TuringArticle.html
Blay Whitby (1997). The Turing Test: AI's Biggest Blind Alley? In: Machines and Thought: The Legacy of Alan Turing. Mind Association Occasional Series, 1. Oxford University Press, USA, pp. 53-62. http://www.sussex.ac.uk/Users/blayw/tt.html

Periodical and Internet Sources Bibliography

The following articles have been selected to supplement the diverse views presented in this chapter.

Marcus du Sautoy, "Can Computers Have True Artificial Intelligence?" BBC News, April 3, 2012.

Alex Fitzpatrick, "Google's AI Just Did Something Nobody Thought Possible," *Time*, January 27, 2016.

Luciano Floridi, "Should We Be Afraid of AI?" Aeon, May 9, 2016.

Ina Fried, "Microsoft Taps the Brainpower of Its Legendary Research Unit in an Artificial Intelligence Push," *Recode*, September 29, 2016.

Luke Muehlhauser, "When Will AI Be Created?" Machine Intelligence Research Institute, May 15, 2013.

Alina Selyukh, "Tech Giants Team Up to Tackle the Ethics of Artificial Intelligence," NPR, September 28, 2016.

Andrew Sheehy, "Superintelligence Is Not Just Possible, but Inevitable," *Forbes*, June 22, 2016.

Vivek Wadhwa, "The Amazing Artificial Intelligence We Were Promised Is Coming, Finally," Washington Post.com, June 17, 2016.

OPPOSING
VIEWPOINTS®
SERIES

CHAPTER 2

| How Could AI Affect
Our Society?

Chapter Preface

B y now we have heard from a few high-profile voices in the intellectual and entrepreneurial communities warning of the dire "existential threat" posed by artificial intelligence. Putting aside these stern admonitions temporarily, we can better gauge how artificial intelligence will unfold if we resist speculation about adversarial relations with our silicon-based robot creations. Rather, to make an educated guess at how AI might look in the future, we can simply examine how our existing economic system allocates resources for AI research, the tasks to which machine intelligence is currently applied, and the interests research and development ultimately serve.

It should come as no surprise that the private sector drives AI research. Silicon-valley tech firms such as Apple, Google, and Facebook, along with startups such as Vicarious, all have enormous proprietary stakes in the fruits of AI research. However, all the so-called AI in use could more properly be called "intelligence augmentation." This is technology meant to enhance human intelligence, not to surpass or supplant it. Intelligence augmentation takes the form of the algorithms that tell us what other television shows we might enjoy based on our viewing habits, or place targeted advertising in our social media feeds. It is enabled by the vast swaths of data that companies are now able to analyze using computers. This proprietary technology is overwhelmingly oriented toward serving the consumer and maximizing profits. For this reason, some observers believe that "AI" is currently just a marketing buzzword, offering little revolutionary benefit to society other than more efficient shopping, at the cost of less privacy.

The trend toward utilizing narrow AI in more and more areas of life may not give us human-level intelligence robots, but it will definitely give us profound changes in the employment market. Opinions are divided on how these changes will affect different classes. Some believe that technology will liberate all humans from most drudgery of labor. Those arguing this view cite previous advances such as the ATM, which theoretically allows human capital to be used more effectively by the banking industry. On the other hand, those who are skeptical of technological utopianism warn of the chance that further automation will create a sector of society that is permanently unemployable. To a society used to seeing identity tied to one's economic value as a producer, such a shift could have many negative consequences. Thus, some observers are trying to reframe our conception of work to suit the future that is on the way.

In conjunction with private defense firms, the military is another huge developer of narrow AI. Based on current practices such as drones, some commentators have speculated that the future of warfare will involve so-called killer robots. Foremost on the minds of many is how to prevent this technology from falling into the wrong hands. Some advocate open-source programs, arguing that free information will create a natural checks and balance system. Others disagree and believe this could give rogue actors a head start to destruction. Weaponized AI in a highly militarized society is perhaps the single greatest threat of this technology, both now and into the foreseeable future.

> *"For those who expect AI and robotics to significantly displace human employment, these displacements seem certain to lead to an increase in income inequality, a continued hollowing out of the middle class, and even riots, social unrest, and/ or the creation of a permanent, unemployable 'underclass.'"*

Opinions Are Divided on Whether Machines Will Replace Workers

Aaron Smith and Janna Anderson

In the research for the following excerpted article, nearly 2,000 experts were asked questions regarding how advancing technology will affect employment. Slightly over half the respondents believed net job creation due to technology will more than offset job loss. On the other hand, just under half the respondents believed a loss of jobs, or even a permanently unemployable class, would result from the automation at the hands of intelligent machines. The pessimists tend to be more critical of capitalism, the optimists more embracing. However, both groups predict major shake-ups in the coming decades. Aaron Smith is a senior researcher at the Pew Research Center's Internet Project, and Prof. Janna Anderson is director of Elon University's Imagining the Internet Center.

"Predictions for the State of AI and Robotics in 2025," Aaron Smith and Janna Anderson, Pew Research Center, August 6, 2014. Reprinted by permission.

As you read, consider the following questions:

1. What recurring argument backs the position that technological advances will create more jobs than it destroys?
2. Do those who claim technology will liberate people from labor tend to question capitalism? Is this a logical flaw?
3. How do those who feel automation will yield a race to the bottom justify their position?

The sizeable majority of experts surveyed for this report envision major advances in robotics and artificial intelligence in the coming decade. In addition to asking them for their predictions about the job market of the future, we also asked them to weigh in on the following question:

> To what degree will AI and robotics be parts of the ordinary landscape of the general population by 2025? Describe which parts of life will change the most as these tools advance and which parts of life will remain relatively unchanged.

These are the themes that emerged from their answers to this question.

AI and robotics will be integrated into nearly every aspect of most people's daily lives

Many respondents see advances in AI and robotics pervading nearly every aspect of daily life by the year 2025—from distant manufacturing processes to the most mundane household activities.

Jeff Jarvis, director of the Tow-Knight Center for Entrepreneurial Journalism at the City University of New York, wrote, "Think 'Intel Inside'. By 2025, artificial intelligence will be built into the algorithmic architecture of countless functions of business and communication, increasing relevance, reducing noise, increasing efficiency, and reducing risk across everything from finding information to making transactions. If robot cars are not yet driving on their own, robotic and intelligent functions will be taking over more of the work of manufacturing and moving."

Vint Cerf, vice president and chief Internet evangelist for Google, responded, "Self-driving cars seem very likely by 2025. Natural language processing will lead to conversational interactions with computer-based systems. Google search is likely to become a dialog rather than a client-server interaction. The Internet of Things will be well under way by this time and interaction with and among a wide range of appliances is predictable. Third party services to manage many of these devices will also be common."

Stowe Boyd, lead researcher for GigaOM Research, predicted, "Pizzas will not be delivered by teenagers hoping for a tip. Food will be raised by robotic vehicles, even in small plot urban farms that will become the norm, since so many people will have lost their jobs to 'bots. Your X-rays will be reviewed by a battery of Watson-grade AIs, and humans will only be pulled in when the machines disagree. Robotic sex partners will be a commonplace, although the source of scorn and division, the way that critics today bemoan selfies as an indicator of all that's wrong with the world."

K.G. Schneider, a university librarian, wrote, "By 2025 AI, robotics, and ubiquitous computing will have snuck into parts of our lives without us understanding to what extent it has happened (much as I just went on a camping trip with a smartphone, laptop, and tablet)."

Lillie Coney, a legislative director specializing in technology policy in the U.S. House of Representatives, replied, "It is not the large things that will make AI acceptable it will be the small things—portable devices that can aid a person or organization in accomplishing desired outcomes well. AI embedded into everyday technology that proves to save time, energy, and stress that will push consumer demand for it."

JP Rangaswami, chief scientist for Salesforce.com, wrote, "Traditional agriculture and manufacturing will both be affected quite heavily, with AI and robotics having greater roles to play at scale, while high-touch 'retro' boutiques will exist for both sectors.

Service sector impact will continue to be lower in relative terms; knowledge/information worker sector impact, on the other hand, will be transformational."

Marc Prensky, director of the Global Future Education Foundation and Institute, wrote, "The penetration of AI and robotics will be close to 100% in many areas. It will be similar to the penetration of cell phones today: over two-thirds of the world now have and use them daily."

Nilofer Merchant, author of a book on new forms of advantage, wrote, "Let me put it this way: my son, who is 10, doesn't think he needs to learn to drive or do grocery shopping because he says he'll just click something to arrive. All the fundamentals of life can and will be automated, from driving to grocery shopping. Chores effectively disappear in terms of time consumption."

A Syracuse University professor and associate dean for research wrote, "Robots and AI are moving beyond simple rules into framed judgment spaces. There will be several spectacular failures (to give voice to the dystopian seers) and so many subtle impacts. I see them in public transport, long-distance driving, traffic routing, and car-to-car interactions. I also see them moving into the built environment through post-market sensor networks reflecting energy monitoring, maintenance for household appliances, and supporting more distributed education. My expectation is that much of medicine will be in the midst of a transformation based on better sensors tied to more powerful analytics."

David Clark, a senior research scientist at MIT's Computer Science and Artificial Intelligence Laboratory, noted that AI is already a part of daily life for many users: "AI methods and techniques are already part of the ordinary landscape. The problem with the term 'AI' is that it is constantly redefined to describe things we don't yet know how to do well with computers. Things like speech recognition (like Siri), image recognition (face recognition in consumer cameras), and the like used to be hard AI problems. As they become practical commercial offerings, they spin off as their own disciplines."

However, some experts sounded a note of concern that the gains from these new advances risk being limited only to those with the financial resources to afford the latest technologies, which may reinforce economic inequality.

The CEO of a professional not-for-profit society responded, "We will have more and more robots and AI in our lives, although I fear the benefits will accrue to the top 1-2% who can afford the gadgets." And an information science professional and leader for a national association wrote, "In terms of day-to-day living, AI and robotics could easily be something that only the 1% can afford or have access to. In fields like medicine, though, advances have the potential to help everyone."

A journalist, editor, and leader of an online news organization wrote, "Typically, this will depend on socioeconomics. The rich will spend almost no time doing things that can be automated; the poor will continue as is, more or less, although with superior communication abilities."

Bill Woodcock, executive director for the Packet Clearing House, responded, "The degree of integration of AI into daily life will depend very much, as it does now, on wealth. The people whose personal digital devices are day-trading for them, and doing the grocery shopping, and sending greeting cards on their behalf, are people who are living a different life than those who are worried about missing a day at one of their three jobs due to being sick, and losing the job, and being unable to feed their children."

These technologies will be integrated so completely as to be nearly invisible to most users most of the time
Depictions of robotics and artificial intelligence in popular culture often lean towards powerful anthropomorphic robots (Transformers, The Terminator) and hulking mainframes with human-like intelligence (HAL in 2001). But many of the experts who responded to this survey expect technology to evolve in the opposite direction, with machine intelligence being hidden deep

in the complex workings of outwardly simple or even invisible devices and digital interactions.

John Markoff, senior writer for the Science section of the New York Times, likens this process to a kind of magic: "Over the next decade the ubiquitous computing era will come into full force. Computers will 'disappear' and ordinary objects will become magic. Significantly, Steve Jobs was the first one to really understand this. But the pace is relentless."

Nishant Shah, a visiting professor at The Centre for Digital Cultures at Leuphana University in Germany, wrote, "The primary function of care robots or companion AIs is to be invisible. They are already ubiquitous in the world that we live in, but largely they work under the surface, and below the networks. Advancements in nanotechnologies and wearable computing are going more in the direction of creating tools that we do not see."

David Organ, CEO of Dotsub, wrote, "The progressive availability of more and more robust AI systems, with deeper predictive power and broader contextual understanding will make them almost invisible. The people who are not specialists of the field will react to their advances being pointed out with a sense of natural acceptance because the progressive arrival of better and better features and performance will have created a sense of familiarity. It will be natural to talk to computers of any shape, and expect them to understand the words, and the meaning, and to establish a dialog leading rapidly to the desired goal."

Elizabeth Albrycht, a senior lecturer in marketing and communications at the Paris School of Business, replied, "By 2025 we may well be witnessing the disappearance of AI and robotics *into* the ordinary landscape as they follow the usual path of technology. First we see it, then it becomes invisible as it integrates into the landscape itself."

The fact that the "invisible" technologies of the future may be doing jobs currently held by human beings was not lost on some respondents:

Jamais Cascio, a writer and futurist specializing in possible futures scenario outcomes, wrote, "By 2025, robots/AI (although likely not 'true' self-aware autonomous constructed intelligence) will start to become background noise in the day-to-day lives of people in the post-industrial world. From self-driving taxis to garbage collectors to autonomous service systems, machines will start to exist in our social space the way that low-paid (often immigrant) human workers do now: visible but ignorable. (To be clear: I'm not celebrating this, I'm just acknowledging it.) We'll know they're there, we'll interact with them in perfunctory ways, but they will less and less often be seen as noticeable."

Olivier Crepin-Leblond, managing director of Global Information Highway Ltd. in London, UK, offered similar thoughts when he predicted that, "…An enormous amount of automata will replace humans—from automated passport gates at border control, to onsite vending machines, automated floor cleaners, window cleaning machines, driving trains, cars etc. Our day-to-day life will remain the same, but those jobs performed in the past by what some call 'invisible people,' will be performed by 'invisible robots.' How many people remember the face of the ticket collector on their train? That's what I mean by 'invisible people.' Now the life of the people performing the work of 'invisible people' will be heavily affected as they'll be out of work. The life of others too: I rely on these 'invisible people' to bring a human face to the world and to my life—a hello, a smile, a thanks."

Driving, transportation, and logistics will experience dramatic changes

Many respondents predicted that self-driving cars will enter the ordinary landscape in a meaningful way within the next decade. **Howard Rheingold**, a pioneering Internet sociologist and self-employed writer, consultant, and educator, expressed his belief that this can only be for the best: "I, for one, welcome our self-driving automobile overlords. How could they possibly do a worse job than the selfish, drugged, drunk, and distracted humans who have turned our roads into bloodbaths for decades?" A self-employed programmer and Web developer offered similar thoughts: "We might wonder how we accepted so many car accidents in 2013 and wonder why we even bothered to perform the necessary but menial task of, say, parking."

Other respondents imagined a future with many more driverless cars, but many fewer truck drivers, delivery people, and taxi operators. **danah boyd**, a research scientist for Microsoft, responded, "There will be a lot more automation but much of it will be as invisible as it is now. So in that sense, yes, it will be part of the ordinary landscape. The biggest change will be to the movement of atoms—food, consumer goods, etc. The majority of the disruption will be at the blue-collar level, and I suspect that the biggest impact will be in warehouses (or 'fulfillment centers')."

Tom Standage, digital editor for The Economist, wrote, "Self-driving vehicles promise to upend existing approaches to car ownership, car design, car sales and insurance, urban planning, logistics, deliveries, taxi services, etc. That will be a big change, as significant as the advent of smartphones." And **Linda Rogers**, the founder of Music Island in Second Life and grant writer for Arts for Children and Youth in Toronto, concurred: "We already see it in grocery scanners, bank machines and can extrapolate from there as automated parking lots add robotic valet service, subway lines no longer require drivers, and garbage pickup services are robot-controlled."

Other respondents envisioned a wide range of impacts that might arise from the driverless car revolution—from the economic to the cultural.

Andrew Rens, chief council at the Shuttleworth Foundation, wrote, "AI and robotics will change the way that Western society thinks about cars. Once control over driving passes to software the romance of cars will diminish. There will be far less cachet in owning large and powerful cars since the riding (rather than driving) experience will be indistinguishable."

Robert Bell of IntelligentCommunity.org responded, "Technology will continue to make things better, faster, cheaper and safer: the impact of self-driving cars alone will be immense in terms of reduced traffic congestion, lower costs for insurance and transport, and driver safety."

A professor at Aoyama Gakuin University in Tokyo, Japan, wrote, "Self-driving cars may change a lot. Car renting and sharing will be far easier and thus more popular, which will be a good thing. On the other hand, spending long hours in cars will be easier (because you can sleep or work or watch a movie while driving), which is not necessarily a good thing."

Intelligent agents will increasingly manage our day-to-day lives and be omnipresent in our homes

As computer intelligence becomes increasingly integrated in daily life, a number of experts expect major changes in the way people manage their households and day-to-day lives.

Hal Varian, chief economist for Google, views the current wave of smartphone-enabled assistants as the tip of the iceberg: "We will rely on personal assistance from devices such as Google Now, Siri, Watson, etc. Much of the interaction will be verbal, so this will look a lot like the Star Trek computer interaction. We will expect computers that we meet to know us and our history of interaction with them. In general, they will infer what we want, and our role is simply to refine and verify that expectation. We will be well on our way to universal access to all human knowledge via the worldwide network of mobile devices and data centers. Day-to-day interaction with devices and data will be by voice. One industry that will be hugely affected is education: what should be people be taught when they can access all human knowledge all the time?"

A CEO for a company that builds intelligent machines wrote, "The creative class by 2025 will have a digital assistant in their work and personal lives who all but replaces what we think of today as administrative help. That entity (actually a collection of distributed software) will answer phones, schedule appointments (handling the logistics far more accurately than any human), manage the care and maintenance of that person's living quarters and work environment, do the shopping and (where appropriate) be responsible for managing that person's financial life."

Frederic Litto, a professor emeritus at the University of Sao Paulo in Brazil, responded, "It will probably be in 'concierge'-type services—that is, everyone's device (be it smartphone, tablet, or Dick-Tracy-on-the-wrist devices) will have built-in applications to remind users of things to be done, and featuring unlimited lists of contacts, past and present, as well as the contents of global and local reference works, model decision-trees, and other handy information devices. Concierge-type services will give citizens greater autonomy in everyday activities, as well as in highly specialized professional activities (like on-the-wrist 'specialist systems' for medical diagnoses)."

A technology policy expert wrote, "Where I think the public will see it more is via mobile devices and home automation. I expect that new construction will include learning thermostats, embedded smoke detectors, smart appliances, automated door locks, etc., all run by apps."

A general manager for Microsoft replied, "Robotics and AI will have a broader role in daily life. We are already seeing trends in home automation and maintenance, for example, that if extrapolated to 2025 at the same development rate will create substantially different experiences in a future-modern home."

Large swathes of the service sector—both online and off—will be impacted

Many experts anticipate that advances in AI and robotics will produce dramatic changes in the service industry by 2025. **Glenn Edens**, a director of research in networking, security, and distributed systems within the Computer Science Laboratory at PARC, a Xerox Company, predicted, "It is likely most consumer services (banking, food, retail, etc.) will move to more and more self-service delivery via automated systems."

Joe Touch, director of the Information Sciences Institute's Postel Center at the University of Southern California, replied, "They will continue to replace certain simple tasks, including, I would expect, mail and package delivery, and will increasingly shift from warehouses to public shopping areas (e.g., restocking shelves, or avoiding the need for bulk shelf displays in stores altogether). Interfaces will increasingly involve speech recognition and vision, interacting with people on more 'human' terms."

An anonymous respondent wrote, "A large portion of service jobs may be taken over by AI—ticket clerks at movie theaters, bank tellers, automated clerks in most service positions. Once we begin to program the software to manage intelligent response to human interaction we may find that simpler tasks may be taken over completely by AI."

Per Ola Kristensson, a lecturer in human-computer interaction at the University of St Andrews, UK, responded, "While automation will be less than perfect by 2025, we are likely to witness a trend in which routine white-collar jobs, such as routine legal work, accounting, and administration, will be replaced by AI tools."

Several experts predicted that most of our online and telephone interactions with customer service "personnel" in the future will be with intelligent algorithms. **Judith Donath**, a fellow at Harvard University's Berkman Center for Internet & Society, responded, "Conversations with intelligent-seeming agents will be far more common. It will be frequently difficult to tell (online at least) if you are speaking/chatting with a person or program—and people will have become accustomed to this and will have ceased to care in many cases. Dealing with a machine will often be more efficient, and many people will come to use the sort of shorthand commands—no greetings or niceties, imperative forms—that they use with AI agents with anyone in a subordinate position."

Thomas Haigh, an information technology historian and associate professor of information studies at the University of Wisconsin, observed, "AI will make it increasingly easy to interface with computer systems in flexible ways. Automated decision making has largely automated fairly complex business processes like credit card applications, and coupled with big data will continue to displace human judgment in routine transactions."

Mary Joyce, an Internet researcher and digital activism consultant, replied, "Customer service, which firms have been trying to automate and outsource to the frustration of customers, are likely to adopt interactive automated customer service agents more sophisticated than current voice-recognition systems."

Advances in AI and robotics will be a boon for the elderly, disabled, and sick

A number of experts surveyed predicted that caring for the sick, elderly, and physically challenged will be revolutionized by advances in robotics.

David Clark, a senior research scientist at MIT's Computer Science and Artificial Intelligence Laboratory, said, "I like to consider questions such as this by asking what problem needs a solution. I believe that one reason the 'smart home' has not taken off so well is that the dumb house is good enough. I think commuting is a problem (so self-driving cars as well as telework will be popular). We will see robots in health care and care of the elderly. But these may not be humanoid robots, but devices designed to work in specialized spaces designed for them."

Jonathan Grudin, principal researcher for Microsoft, responded, "I expect more robotic assistance for the elderly and infirm, because the demands are manageable and the need is increasing."

Gary Kreps, professor of communication and director of the Center for Health and Risk Communication at George Mason University, wrote, "Smart interactive virtual human agents will be a common part of modern life, providing the public with access to relevant information and support wherever they are and whenever they need help. This will be particularly important in providing consumers with access to relevant health information and support for making important health promotion decisions and guiding self-care and care for loved ones at home. This will improve the quality of self- and other-care, as well as enhance adherence with health regimens in the future."

The head of the department of communication at a top U.S. university wrote, "The low-hanging fruit for AI and robotics are areas of labor that still involve high degrees of routine. Special areas of need in the developed world involve domestic assistance for aging populations and other vulnerable groups."

Daren C. Brabham, assistant professor at the Annenberg School for Communication & Journalism, University of Southern California, says these developments could help expand health coverage in hard-to-reach populations: "I see robotics/AI taking a stronger hold in medicine, both in medical research and testing and in doctor-patient interactions. On this latter point, basic telemedicine applications/robots will serve a significant portion of healthcare needs for rural and poor populations by 2025, with robot-doc-in-a-box pods dispersed throughout the country that can automatically take blood pressure, draw blood, and other simple diagnostic procedures."

The CEO of a software technology company and active participant in Internet standards development, responded, "Hopefully one of the areas where this will have most impact is the medical field—this is an area where there are high costs, a shortage of highly skilled people and a growing demand for advanced and complex services."

Janet Kornblum, a self-employed media trainer and journalist, observed, "Robotics is already a part of our landscape. Medically, many of us will use intelligent devices that help us function, be they smart replacements for little reminders that tell us when to take our pills, etc. Will robots be caring for us? Maybe. I think medical robots will lead the way."

Larry Magid, a technology journalist and an Internet safety advocate, responded, "People won't have to drive cars unless they want to, and senior citizens and people with disabilities will be able to live more independently."

Minority viewpoint: expect these changes to be gradual and incremental

Although most of our respondents expect dramatic advances in AI and robotics in the coming decade, some expect that these changes will occur much more gradually.

Seth Finkelstein, a programmer, consultant, and EFF Pioneer of the Electronic Frontier Award winner responded, "We're still a very long way from 'AI' as generally seen in the movies, i.e. humanoid robots. A picture of a city street scene of 2013 doesn't look too different from 50 years ago. Well, there are all the people looking into handheld little rectangles, but still, for many years there were people walking along with small oblong boxes pressed to their ears. It's when you consider the difference between what they're carrying, the smartphone versus the transistor radio, that the magnitude of the change is located."

A program director focusing on ICT standards policy, Internet Governance and other issues wrote, "It will still be limited. Although we can already do some pretty cool stuff, there will still be plenty of kinks and bugs and vulnerabilities that need to be resolved before market confidence will be widespread."

The former chair of an IETF working group wrote, "Change will continue to be pretty gradual in the next 12 years. AI and robotics are making great strides but will not suddenly take over a lot of domestic / household functions. The areas that border on factory automation are the candidates for change—perhaps low skill assembly and clothing fabrication jobs will be affected next."

A professor at a major U.S. business school responded, "Automated cars will not make it into use—this is way harder than anybody is letting on in public conversation. IBM's Watson was so specialized to one application that it will take enormous effort to reapply it to anything else. We will see advances in little things, like better phone trees, and smarter applications online, but nothing dramatic."

The principal architect at an enterprise computing firm wrote, "Partial solutions will dominate—parking aids, automatic mowers and the like. People underestimate the value and convenience of cheap labor."

An executive at an Internet top-level domain name operator replied, "Considering the percentage of the U.S. population that remains offline to this day, we shouldn't get ahead of ourselves in predicting some kind of *I, Robot*-type world within 10 years—which is less time than the commercial Internet has been available."

"Out of the box" responses

Along with the major themes highlighted above, several experts made thought-provoking predictions about the future of AI and robotics that did not fit cleanly into any of these major categories. Among the more interesting ideas proposed:

Warfare and police work will be increasingly mechanized

Several experts expressed concerns about increased mechanization of warfare, surveillance, and police work. **Marc Rotenberg**, president of the Electronic Privacy Information Center (EPIC), noted, "You will see early versions of RoboCop on city streets. Looking at the current evolution of surveillance drones we can anticipate that that they will have the ability to interpret sound and images. They will also sense chemical compositions to help identify explosive and other harmful elements. They will likely have both infrared detection as well as the ability to see through solid materials and detect heat signatures. They will certainly have facial recognition capabilities and be integrated with a national biometric center. An interesting question is whether they will also have non-lethal weapons, such as tasers. Several incidents of attacks on robots will be reported."

Jamais Cascio, a writer and futurist specializing in possible futures scenario outcomes, expressed similar concerns: "The big exception [to the increased use of AI and robotics] will be in the world of civic response and emergency drones, whether for police work, fire suppression, emergency responders, climate mitigation, and the like. These will be designed to be visible, imposing (especially if they're needed to assist civic authorities), and a little scary—imagine autonomous fire trucks."

Increased automation will spark a "machine free" movement
Andrew Rens, chief council at the Shuttleworth Foundation, wrote, "The rise of AI and robots will also likely change extreme sports and outdoor pursuits not by increased reliance on AI and robotics but by provoking a movement to purge extreme sports of them. Extreme sports and outdoor pursuits such as hunting are one area of life that encourages immersion in the natural world, self-reliance, and human excellence. As other areas of life become increasingly dominated by machines that are faster, more accurate, and more reliable than humans, outdoor pursuits and extreme sports will become increasingly valuable to a substantial minority as they seek to carve out space from a frenetically connected world. The perception of extreme sports and outdoor pursuits as a machine-free zone will provoke debate about the ethics of relying on machines. A significant minority of sportspeople will attempt complete human self-reliance, even refusing current technologies such as GPS except in emergencies."

The nature of memory and imagination will change
Tiffany Shlain, filmmaker, host of the AOL series *The Future Starts Here*, and founder of The Webby Awards, responded, "The parts of life that will change most will be our sense of memory and interactions with new ideas. We will have robotic aids to help us remember facts, memories and access to ideas that will give our minds amplified abilities. Everyone human on the planet who wants to be connected will definitely be connected by 2025. This intersection and recall of diverse ideas will have led to great innovation. What will not change—is our human desire for authentic connection and eye contact."

The world will contain more "magic"

A research scientist working at a major search engine company responded, "There will be more 'magic' in the world. I mean this in the sense that more actions will be taken for us, to us, by our systems that will not have explanations attached or perceivable reasons why they're being taken. Example: recommender systems will become everyday interactions multiple times per day. In many cases, even the software engineers have no idea, really, why a particular recommendation is being made. That's surprising, and magical. You decide if it's net good or not. Opinions will be split."

> "In the 19th century machines competed with human brawn. Now machines are competing with human brain. Robots combine brain and brawn. We are facing the prospect of being completely out-competed by our own creations."

Intelligent Machines Will Make Human Workers Obsolete

Moshe Y. Vardi

In the following viewpoint, Moshe Y. Vardi speculates about a future in which machines become our intellectual and physical equals or superiors. Vardi is less concerned about the coming singularity than he is about robots taking work and other meaningful activities away from humans in the near future. Furthermore, he finds the various arguments advanced to quell his fears unconvincing. Like many observers of AI, his ultimate message is one of caution. He believes that there is little chance of slowing technological advancement but recommends we ponder the consequences of this before going forward too rashly. Moshe Y. Vardi is a professor of computational engineering at Rice University.

"The Consequences of Machine Intelligence," by Moshe Y. Vardi, article originally published by the Atlantic Monthly, October 2012. Reprinted by permission.

As you read, consider the following questions:

1. How does the author present the singularity and the "singularitarians"?
2. Does the author think machines will ever fully replace humans in the workplace?
3. What is "relinquishment"? Does the author think this is a practical approach to machine intelligence?

The question of what happens when machines get to be as intelligent as and even more intelligent than people seems to occupy many science-fiction writers. The Terminator movie trilogy, for example, featured Skynet, a self-aware artificial intelligence that served as the trilogy's main villain, battling humanity through its Terminator cyborgs. Among technologists, it is mostly "Singularitarians" who think about the day when machine will surpass humans in intelligence. The term "singularity" as a description for a phenomenon of technological acceleration leading to "machine-intelligence explosion" was coined by the mathematician Stanislaw Ulam in 1958, when he wrote of a conversation with John von Neumann concerning the "ever accelerating progress of technology and changes in the mode of human life, which gives the appearance of approaching some essential singularity in the history of the race beyond which human affairs, as we know them, could not continue." More recently, the concept has been popularized by the futurist Ray Kurzweil, who pinpointed 2045 as the year of singularity. Kurzweil has also founded Singularity University and the annual Singularity Summit.

It is fair to say, I believe, that Singularitarians are not quite in the mainstream. Perhaps it is due to their belief that by 2045 humans will also become immortal and be able to download their consciousness to computers. It was, therefore, quite surprising when in 2000, Bill Joy, a very mainstream technologist as co-founder of Sun Microsystems, wrote an article entitled "Why the Future Doesn't Need Us" for *Wired* magazine. "Our most powerful 21st-century technologies—robotics, genetic engineering, and nanotech—are threatening to make humans an endangered species," he wrote. Joy's article was widely noted when it appeared, but it seems to have made little impact.

It is in the context of the Great Recession that people started noticing that while machines have yet to exceed humans in intelligence, they are getting intelligent enough to have a major impact on the job market. In their 2011 book, *Race Against The Machine: How the Digital Revolution is Accelerating Innovation, Driving Productivity, and Irreversibly Transforming Employment and the Economy* authors Erik Brynjolfsson and Andrew McAfee, argued that "technological progress is accelerating innovation even as it leaves many types of workers behind." Indeed, over the past 30 years, as we saw the personal computer morph into tablets, smartphones, and cloud computing, we also saw income inequality grow worldwide. While the loss of millions of jobs over the past few years has been attributed to the Great Recession, whose end is not yet in sight, it now seems that technology-driven productivity growth is at least a major factor. Such concerns have gone mainstream in the past year, with articles in newspapers and magazines carrying titles such as "More Jobs Predicted for Machines, Not People," "Marathon Machine: Unskilled Workers Are Struggling to Keep Up With Technological Change," "It's a Man vs. Machine Recovery," and "The Robots Are Winning."

Early AI pioneers were brimming with optimism about the possibilities of machine intelligence. Alan Turing's 1950 paper, "Computing Machinery and Intelligence" is perhaps best known for his proposal of an "Imitation Game," known today as "the Turing Test," as an operational definition for machine intelligence. But the main focus of the 1950 paper is actually not the Imitation Game but the possibility of machine intelligence. Turing carefully analyzed and rebutted arguments against machine intelligence. He also stated his belief that we will see machine intelligence by the end of the 20th century, writing "I believe that at the end of the century the use of words and general educated opinion will have altered so much that one will be able to speak of machines thinking without expecting to be contradicted."

While we now know that Turing was too optimistic on the timeline, AI's inexorable progress over the past 50 years suggests that Herbert Simon was right when he wrote in 1956 "machines will be capable ... of doing any work a man can do." I do not expect this to happen in the very near future, but I do believe that by 2045 machines will be able to do if not any work that humans can do, then a very significant fraction of the work that humans can do. Bill Joy's question deserves therefore not to be ignored: Does the future need us? By this I mean to ask, if machines are capable of doing almost any work humans can do, what will humans do? I have been getting various answers to this question, but I find none satisfying.

A typical answer to my raising this question is to tell me that I am a Luddite. (Luddism is defined as distrust or fear of the inevitable changes brought about by new technology.) This is an ad hominem attack that does not deserve a serious answer.

We are facing the prospect of being completely out-competed by our own creations.

A more thoughtful answer is that technology has been destroying jobs since the start of the Industrial Revolution, yet new jobs are continually created. The AI Revolution, however, is different than the Industrial Revolution. In the 19th century machines competed with human brawn. Now machines are competing with human brain. Robots combine brain and brawn. We are facing the prospect of being completely out-competed by our own creations. Another typical answer is that if machines will do all of our work, then we will be free to pursue leisure activities. The economist John Maynard Keynes addressed this issue already in 1930, when he wrote, "The increase of technical efficiency has been taking place faster than we can deal with the problem of labour absorption." Keynes imagined 2030 as a time in which most people worked only 15 hours a week, and would occupy themselves mostly with leisure activities.

I do not find this to be a promising future. First, if machines can do almost all of our work, then it is not clear that even 15 weekly hours of work will be required. Second, I do not find the prospect of leisure-filled life appealing. I believe that work is essential to human well-being. Third, our economic system would have to undergo a radical restructuring to enable billions of people to live lives of leisure. Unemployment rate in the US is currently under 9 percent and is considered to be a huge problem.

Finally, people tell me that my concerns apply only to a future that is so far away that we need not worry about it. I find this answer to be unacceptable. 2045 is merely a generation away from us. We cannot shirk responsibility from concerns for the welfare of the next generation.

In 2000, Bill Joy advocated a policy of relinquishment—"to limit development of the technologies that are too dangerous, by limiting our pursuit of certain kinds of knowledge." I am not sure I am ready to go that far, but I do believe that just because technology can do good, it does not mean that more technology is always better. Turing was what we call today a "techno-enthusiast," writing in 1950 that "we may hope that machines will eventually compete with men in all purely intellectual fields ... we can see plenty there that needs to be done." But his incisive analysis about the possibility of machine intelligence was not accompanied by an analysis of the consequences of machine intelligences. It is time, I believe, to put the question of these consequences squarely on the table. We cannot blindly pursue the goal of machine intelligence without pondering its consequences.

> *"We will soon be looking at hordes of citizens of zero economic value. Figuring out how to deal with the impacts of this development will be the greatest challenge facing free market economies in this century."*

The Workforce of the Future Must Adapt to More Robots and Fewer Jobs

William H. Davidow and Michael S. Malone

In the following viewpoint, Bill Davidow and Michael S. Malone predict that computer intelligence will advance far faster than Industrial Revolution–era machines. This spells trouble for workers across the world, as companies worldwide replace human workers with robots. Even skilled professional areas such as medicine employ machines instead of humans. This will greatly impact the value of work, now and in the future. How we deal with this paradigm shift in human labor and its meaning, for better or for worse, is an open question. William H. Davidow is a high-technology industry executive and has been a venture investor for more than thirty years, and Michael S. Malone has covered Silicon Valley and high tech for more than thirty years.

"What Happens to Society When Robots Replace Workers?" William H. Davidow and Michael S. Malone, *Harvard Business Review,* December 10, 2014. Reprinted by permission.

As you read, consider the following questions:

1. What are some of the ways in which technology is already displacing human workers?
2. How does commentator David Brooks recommend we deal with the encroaching automation of labor?
3. Do the authors share Brooks's view? How does their view differ?

The technologies of the past, by replacing human muscle, increased the value of human effort—and in the process drove rapid economic progress. Those of the future, by substituting for man's senses and brain, will accelerate that process—but at the risk of creating millions of citizens who are simply unable to contribute economically, and with greater damage to an already declining middle class.

Estimates of general rates of technological progress are always imprecise, but it is fair to say that, in the past, progress came more slowly. Henry Adams, the historian, measured technological progress by the power generated from coal, and estimated that power output doubled every ten years between 1840 and 1900, a compounded rate of progress of about 7% per year. The reality was probably much less. For example, in 1848, the world record for rail speed reached 60 miles per hour. A century later, commercial aircraft could carry passengers at speeds approaching 600 miles per hour, a rate of progress of only about 2% per year.

By contrast, progress today comes rapidly. Consider the numbers for information storage density in computer memory. Between 1960 and 2003, those densities increased by a factor of five *million*, at times progressing at a rate of 60% per year. At the same time, true to Moore's Law, semiconductor technology has been progressing at a 40% rate for more than 50 years. These rates of progress are embedded in the creation of intelligent machines, from robots to automobiles to drones, that will soon dominate the global economy—and in the process drive down the value of human labor with astonishing speed.

This is why we will soon be looking at hordes of citizens of zero economic value. Figuring out how to deal with the impacts of this development will be the greatest challenge facing free market economies in this century.

If you doubt the march of worker-replacing technology, look at Foxconn, the world's largest contract manufacturer. It employs more than one million workers in China. In 2011, the company installed 10,000 robots, called Foxbots. Today, the company is installing them at a rate of 30,000 per year. Each robot costs about $20,000 and is used to perform routine jobs such as spraying, welding, and assembly. On June 26, 2013, Terry Gou, Foxconn's CEO, told his annual meeting that "We have over one million workers. In the future we will add one million robotic workers." This means, of course, that the company will avoid hiring those next million human workers.

Just imagine what a Foxbot will soon be able to do if Moore's Law holds steady and we continue to see performance leaps of 40% per year. Baxter, a $22,000 robot that just got a software upgrade, is being produced in quantities of 500 per year. A few years from now, a much smarter Baxter produced in quantities of 10,000 might cost less than $5,000. At that price, even the lowest-paid workers in the least developed countries might not be able to compete.

To be sure, technological progress has always displaced workers. But it also has created new opportunities for human employment, at an even a faster rate. This time, things may be very different—especially as the Internet of Things takes the human factor out of so many transactions and decisions. The "Second Economy" (the term used by economist Brian Arthur to describe the portion of the economy where computers transact business only with other computers) is upon us. It is, quite simply, the virtual economy, and one of its main byproducts is the replacement of workers with intelligent machines powered by sophisticated code. This booming Second Economy is brimming with optimistic entrepreneurs, and already spawning a new generation of billionaires. In fact, the booming Second Economy will probably drive much of the economic growth in the coming decades.

And here is the even more sobering news: Arthur speculates that in a little more than ten years, 2025, this Second Economy may be as large as the original "first" economy was in 1995—about $7.6 trillion. If the Second Economy does achieve that rate of growth, it will be replacing the work of approximately 100 million workers. To put that number in perspective, the current total employed civilian labor force today is 146 million. A sizeable fraction of those replaced jobs will be made up by new ones in the Second Economy. But not all of them. Left behind may be as many as 40 million citizens of no economic value in the U.S alone. The dislocations will be profound.

Suppose, today, that the robots and smart machines of the Second Economy are only capable of doing the work of a person of average intelligence—that is, an IQ of 100. Imagine that the technology in those machines continues to improve at the current rate. Suppose further that this rate of technological progress raises the IQ of these machines by 1.5 points per year. By 2025 these machines will have an IQ greater than 90% of the U.S. population. That 15 point increase in IQ over ten years would put another 50 million jobs within reach of smart machines.

Impossible? In fact, the vanguard of those 115-point IQ machines is already here. In certain applications, the minds of highly educated MD's are no longer needed. In 2013, the FDA approved Johnson & Johnson's Sedasys machine, which delivers propofol to sedate patients without the need for an anesthesiologist. An emerging field in radiology is computer-aided diagnosis (CADx). And a recent study published by the Royal Society showed that computers performed more consistently in identifying radiolucency (the appearance of dark images) than radiologists almost by a factor of ten.

Politicians, economists, and scientists might debate these particular estimates, but to do so is to miss the larger point.

Machine intelligence is already having a major effect on the value of work—and for major segments of the population, human value is now being set by the cost of equivalent machine intelligence.

The challenge now is to keep up with 40% to 60% rates of progress … when even a genius like Henry Adams despaired of keeping up with just a 7% rate.

The simplistic policy answer is better training. But at this pace of change, improving the educational system will be perpetually too little and too late. Likewise, artificially boosting the minimum wage will only hasten the reckoning by subsidizing job replacement by intelligent machines. David Brooks has suggested that the government should aggressively build infrastructure, "reduce its generosity to people who are not working but increase its support for people who are," consider moving to a progressive consumption tax, and "doubling down on human capital, from early education programs to community colleges and beyond." But even if his program were effectively and aggressively implemented, it might keep up with a 40% rate of progress for only a little while.

Meanwhile, Brooks's solutions will lead only to bigger government and greater command and control. And it is difficult to imagine how such a sluggish government system could keep up with such a rapid rate of change when it can barely do so now.

Ultimately, we need a new, individualized, *cultural*, approach to the meaning of work and the purpose of life. Otherwise, people will find a solution—human beings always do—but it may not be the one for which we began this technological revolution.

> *"We need to work out how to build AI systems that result in greater prosperity within society, even for those put out of work."*

AI Should Be Designed to Benefit All of Society

Toby Walsh

In the following viewpoint, Toby Walsh discusses efforts to curtail the potentially dangerous sides of AI, while encouraging equal sharing in its social benefits. One such step is an open letter, which the author notes he has signed. This letter urges developers to take the economic and social consequences of AI into account. Although the author identifies a few issues that are more immediately pressing than AI, he, too, is concerned with killer robots and an emerging superintelligence. However, due to the complexity of the human brain, he believes general AI will not arise for quite some time. Toby Walsh is a professor and research group leader for the optimisation research group Data61.

As you read, consider the following questions:

1. What does the "open letter for AI" recommend?
2. What are some of the issues raised by advancing AI technology?
3. How does the author suggest we deal with these?

S ome of the biggest players in Artificial Intelligence (AI) have joined together calling for any research to focus on the benefits we can reap from AI "while avoiding potential pitfalls." Research into AI continues to seek out new ways to develop technologies that can take on tasks currently performed by humans, but it's not without criticisms and concerns.

I am not sure the famous British theoretical physicist Stephen Hawking does irony but it was somewhat ironic that he recently welcomed the arrival of the smarter predictive computer software that controls his speech by warning us that:

> The development of full artificial intelligence could spell the end of the human race.

Of course, Hawking is not alone in this view. The serial entrepreneur and technologist Elon Musk also warned last year that:

> [...] we should be very careful about artificial intelligence. If I had to guess at what our biggest existential threat is, it's probably that.

Both address an issue that taps into deep, psychological fears that have haunted mankind for centuries. What happens if our creations eventually cause our own downfall? This fear is expressed in stories like Mary Shelley's Frankenstein.

An open letter for AI

In response to such concerns, an open letter has just been signed by top AI researchers in industry and academia (as well as by Hawking and Musk).

OPEN LETTER: RESEARCH PRIORITIES

As capabilities in [AI] and others cross the threshold from laboratory research to economically valuable technologies, a virtuous cycle takes hold whereby even small improvements in performance are worth large sums of money, prompting greater investments in research. There is now a broad consensus that AI research is progressing steadily, and that its impact on society is likely to increase. The potential benefits are huge, since everything that civilization has to offer is a product of human intelligence; we cannot predict what we might achieve when this intelligence is magnified by the tools AI may provide, but the eradication of disease and poverty are not unfathomable. Because of the great potential of AI, it is important to research how to reap its benefits while avoiding potential pitfalls.

The progress in AI research makes it timely to focus research not only on making AI more capable, but also on maximizing the societal benefit of AI. Such considerations motivated the AAAI 2008-09 Presidential Panel on Long-Term AI Futures and other projects on AI impacts, and constitute a significant expansion of the field of AI itself, which up to now has focused largely on techniques that are neutral with respect to purpose. We recommend expanded research aimed at ensuring that increasingly capable AI systems are robust and beneficial: our AI systems must do what we want them to do. The attached research priorities document gives many examples of such research directions that can help maximize the societal benefit of AI. This research is by necessity interdisciplinary, because it involves both society and AI. It ranges from economics, law and philosophy to computer security, formal methods and, of course, various branches of AI itself.

"Autonomous Weapons: An Open Letter from AI and Robotics Researchers," Future of Life Institute, July 28, 2015.

Signatures include those of the president of the Association for the Advancement of Artificial Intelligence, the founders of AI startups DeepMind and Vicarious, and well-known researchers at Google, Microsoft, Stanford and elsewhere.

In the interests of full disclosure, mine is also one of the early signatures on the list, which continues to attract more support by the day.

The open letter argues that there is now a broad consensus that AI research is progressing steadily and its impact on society is likely to increase.

For this reason, the letter concludes we need to start to research how to ensure that increasingly capable AI systems are robust (in their behaviours) and beneficial (to humans). For example, we need to work out how to build AI systems that result in greater prosperity within society, even for those put out of work.

The letter includes a link to a document outlining some interdisciplinary research priorities that should be tackled in advance of developing artificial intelligence. These include short-term priorities such as optimising the economic benefits and long-term priorities such as being able to verify the formal properties of AI systems.

The AI threat to society

Hollywood has provided many memorable visions of the threat AI might pose to society, from Arthur C. Clarke's 2001: A Space Odyssey through Robocop and Terminator to recent movies such as Her and Transcendence, all of which paint a dystopian view of a future transformed by AI.

My opinion (and one many of my colleagues share) is that AI that might threaten our society's future is likely still some way off.

AI researchers have been predicting it will take another 30 or 40 years now for the last 30 or 40 years. And if you ask most of them today, they (as I) will still say it is likely to take another 30 or 40 years.

Making computers behave intelligently is a tough scientific nut to crack. The human brain is the most complex system we know of by orders of magnitude. Replicating the sort of intelligence that humans display will likely require significant advances in AI.

The human brain does all its magic with just 20 watts of power. This is a remarkable piece of engineering.

Other risks to society

There are also more imminent dangers facing mankind such as climate change or the ongoing global financial crisis. These need immediate attention.

The Future of Humanity Institute at the University of Oxford has a long list of threats besides AI that threaten our society including:

- nanotechnology
- biotechnology
- resource depletion
- overpopulation

This doesn't mean that there are not aspects of AI that need attention in the near future.

The AI debate for the future

The Campaign to Stop Killer Robots is advancing the debate on whether we need to ban fully autonomous weapons.

I am organising a debate on this topic at the next annual conference of the Association for the Advancement of Artificial Intelligence later this month in Austin, Texas, in the US.

Steve Goose, director of Human Rights Watch's Arms Division, will speak for a ban, while Ron Arkin, an American roboticist and robo-ethicist, will argue against it.

Another issue that requires more immediate attention is the impact that AI will have on the nature of work. How does society adapt to more automation and fewer people needed to work?

If we can get this right, we could remove much of the drudgery from our lives. If we get it wrong, the increasing inequalities documented by the French economist Thomas Piketty will only get worse.

We will discuss all these issues and more at the first International Workshop on AI and Ethics, also being held in the US within the AAAI Conference on Artificial Intelligence.

It's important we start to have these debates now, not just to avoid the potential pitfalls, but to construct a future where AI improves the world for all of us.

"The continued progress of AI thus poses a new framework for thinking about the relevance of education. It would be a mistake to spend too much time focusing narrowly on skills and content areas that are quickly being sidelined by technology."

AI Will Change How We Learn—And What We Need to Learn

Anya Kamenetz

The following viewpoint examines the impact of Artificial Intelligence on education. Anya Kamenetz begins by noting some recent advances in computer learning. For example, Google has already built a computer that can win the Asian game Go, which is thought to be even more complex than chess. Not surprisingly, educational corporations such as Pearson are currently developing AI tools. The knowledge and skills we need to be successful will change significantly as AI transforms the labor market. However Kamenetz is concerned that educational AI could reinforce existing inequalities. Anya Kamenetz is NPR's lead blogger for education.

As you read, consider the following questions:

1. What types of AI educational tools are currently in development?
2. As labor becomes more and more automated, what job and personal skills does the author think will become most valuable?
3. What problems could arise from the use AI in education?

An artificially intelligent computer system built by Google has just beaten the world's best human, Lee Sedol of South Korea, at an ancient strategy game called Go. Go originated in Asia about 2,500 years ago and is considered many, many times more complex than chess, which fell to AI back in 1997.

And here's what's really crazy. Google's programmers didn't explicitly teach AlphaGo to play the game. Instead, they built a sort of model brain called as a neural network that learned how to play Go by itself.

As NPR's Geoff Brumfiel reported last week:

> The Google program, known as Alpha Go, actually learned the game without much human help. It started by studying a database of about 100,000 human matches, and then continued by playing against itself millions of times.
>
> As it went, it reprogrammed itself and improved. This type of self-learning program is known as a neural network, and it's based on theories of how the human brain works.

Here at NPR Ed, our mission is to cover how learning happens. The advent of computer systems that "learn" surely falls into this category.

And it poses some fascinating questions. First: What could AI technologies do for human education? Second: How should human education respond to the challenges posed by AI?

To the first question, Pearson, the world's largest education company, has just issued a pamphlet from its research division titled Intelligence Unleashed: An argument for AI in Education.

I spoke to Laurie Forcier, one of the authors. She told me that existing computer systems can already provide some of the benefits of one-on-one tutoring. They can also facilitate and moderate group discussions and simulate complex environments for the purpose of learning.

The Pearson report predicts software that will bring helpful feedback in an instant about students' progress, their knowledge state and even their state of mind—eliminating the need to stop and give a standardized test.

On a more futuristic, somewhat creepier note, Forcier and her co-authors also suggest the development of something called a "lifelong learning companion." This is a concept first introduced by early AI researchers decades ago.

Like an imaginary friend, learning companions would accompany students—asking questions, providing encouragement, offering suggestions and connections to resources, helping you talk through difficulties. Over time, the companion would "learn" what you know, what interests you, and what kind of learner you are.

With all its data in the cloud, accessible by phone or laptop, it could follow you from school to soccer practice to internship to college and beyond, and be a valuable record of learning in all contexts. Maybe your learning companion could even write you a letter of recommendation that could serve as a credential.

"Why is the pamphlet called, 'an argument for AI in education' ?" I asked Forcier. "Who's arguing against it?"

She said that, of course, there are fears about AI being used to replace human teachers. Although the pamphlet states "Teachers— alongside learners and parents—should be central to the design of AIEd tools, and the ways that they are used," it also talks about using AI to address teacher shortages, especially where subject matter expertise is missing.

And here we slam right into the second question: How should human education best respond to the challenges, even the threats, posed by AI?

The Open Letter: Autonomous Weapons

Many arguments have been made for and against autonomous weapons, for example that replacing human soldiers by machines is good by reducing casualties for the owner but bad by thereby lowering the threshold for going to battle. The key question for humanity today is whether to start a global AI arms race or to prevent it from starting. If any major military power pushes ahead with AI weapon development, a global arms race is virtually inevitable, and the endpoint of this technological trajectory is obvious: autonomous weapons will become the Kalashnikovs of tomorrow. Unlike nuclear weapons, they require no costly or hard-to-obtain raw materials, so they will become ubiquitous and cheap for all significant military powers to mass-produce. It will only be a matter of time until they appear on the black market and in the hands of terrorists, dictators wishing to better control their populace, warlords wishing to perpetrate ethnic cleansing, etc. Autonomous weapons are ideal for tasks such as assassinations, destabilizing nations, subduing populations and selectively killing a particular ethnic group. We therefore believe that a military AI arms race would not be beneficial for humanity. There are many ways in which AI can make battlefields safer for humans, especially civilians, without creating new tools for killing people.

Just as most chemists and biologists have no interest in building chemical or biological weapons, most AI researchers have no interest in building AI weapons—and do not want others to tarnish their field by doing so, potentially creating a major public backlash against AI that curtails its future societal benefits. Indeed, chemists and biologists have broadly supported international agreements that have successfully prohibited chemical and biological weapons, just as most physicists supported the treaties banning space-based nuclear weapons and blinding laser weapons.

"Autonomous Weapons: An Open Letter From AI and Robotics Researchers, Future of Life Institute, July 28, 2015.

Because, when computer systems aren't winning at chess, *Jeopardy* or Go, they're working. They're booking appointments, preparing legal documents, helping you file your taxes—jobs that used to be done by humans with at least a little bit of education.

The World Economic Forum recently projected that automation will eliminate at least 5 million jobs worldwide by 2020.

The continued progress of AI thus poses a new framework for thinking about the relevance of education. It would be a mistake to spend too much time focusing narrowly on skills and content areas that are quickly being sidelined by technology.

In other words, in a world where computers are taking more and more of the jobs, what is it that humans most need to learn? It probably isn't primarily memorizing facts or figures, or simple rules for problem solving.

An immediate answer is that more of us need to get better at building and interacting with software tools. That's why President Obama, for example, has called for all U.S. students to be exposed to computer science.

A second answer is complementary to the first. Responding to the AlphaGo victory, Geoff Colvin, an editor for *Fortune* magazine and the author of a book about human capabilities, wrote in The New York Times:

> Advancing technology will profoundly change the nature of high-value human skills and that is threatening, but we aren't doomed. The skills of deep human interaction, the abilities to manage the exchanges that occur only between people, will only become more valuable.

As examples, Colvin names empathy, managing collaboration in groups and storytelling—that is, creative communication.

That sounds a whole lot like the growing movement in education to focus on building social and emotional competencies.

This takes us back to the "argument" about AI in education, though. It's most likely that human teachers are best at teaching human students how to manage what Colvin called "the exchanges that occur only between people."

But to beat people out for jobs, computer systems don't necessarily have to be better at those jobs. (Have you had a great experience with an automated phone menu recently?) Because they work, more or less, for free.

So one great fear when it comes to the Pearson vision of AIEd is that we reproduce existing inequalities. Some students get individualized attention from highly skilled human teachers who use the best learning software available to inform their practice. Other students get less face time with lower-skilled teachers plus TutorBots that imperfectly simulate human interaction.

It's a genuine human challenge, one that's a lot more complex than any game.

Periodical and Internet Sources Bibliography

The following articles have been selected to supplement the diverse views presented in this chapter.

Thomas G. Dietterich, "Benefits and Risks of Artificial Intelligence," Medium, January 22, 2015.

Daniel Faggella, "Exploring the Risks of Artificial Intelligence," Tech Crunch, March 21, 2016.

Jack Karsten and Darrell M. West, "How Robots, Artificial Intelligence, and Machine Learning Will Affect Employment and Public Policy," The Brookings Institution, October 26, 2015.

Tanya Lewis, "Artificial Intelligence: Friendly or Frightening?" LiveScience, December 4, 2014.

John Markoff, "Study to Examine Effects of Artificial Intelligence," *New York Times*, December 15, 2014.

Nature, "Anticipating Artificial Intelligence," April 26, 2016.

Danny Palmer, "UK Looks at Impact of AI and Robotics on Jobs and Society," ZDNet, March 24, 2016.

The Wall Street Journal, "What's Next for Artificial Intelligence," June 14, 2016.

OPPOSING
VIEWPOINTS®
SERIES

CHAPTER 3

Should Machines Be Built Like Humans?

Chapter Preface

F ashioning a machine that meaningfully replicates human thought and action is almost unfathomable at the time of this writing. As it turns out, engineering a robotic equivalent to the human brain takes more than an equivalent amount of "pentaflops"—a unit of measure for high levels of processing power. Although the field of brain emulation is relatively new, some researchers are reporting that they can map and replicate all the connections that make up a rodent brain. If this is possible to do now so the argument goes, it is simply a matter of time until we have the processing power and theoretical models to do the same for a human brain. At that point, we will have the functional machine equivalent of human-level intelligence, according to the optimists working on brain emulation.

Citing a qualitative, potentially unbridgeable conceptual gap between organic life and machine intelligence, certain AI skeptics disagree with this approach entirely. On the extreme end of this line of thought, one commentator even asserts that simple bacteria exercise agency, purpose, and autonomy in the world to a far greater degree than even our most advanced computers. To this author, there is something unique about and perhaps inherent to the proteins and molecular structures of carbon-based life that cannot be reproduced artificially. With respect to the human experience, others agree that our embodiment, or specifically, the deep patterns of knowledge that come from having a body and all that comes with it such as digestive, respiratory, and reproductive systems makes machine intelligence wholly unlike human life, no matter how complex AI systems evolve to become.

To some, the question of whether we should build machines like humans is easily answered—we should not, because we cannot. While the objections of these skeptics must be duly noted, we should also take into account unimaginable leaps in future technology and the feats such leaps could enable. Perhaps at some point, every system of both the human brain and body can be analyzed and synthesized. Although the product of this technology might lack a body, it could theoretically still approximate all the effects of these various systems working in tandem.

Unfortunately, debate about the future can easily fall into idle speculation. To bear on the present, we might reframe the question: if we could build machines to behave like humans, what kind of humans would we use as templates? This leads up toward a discussion of what we value. In practical terms, what we value will greatly influence the current direction of AI research. For example, those who feel emotional intelligence is essential will seek ways of endowing our intelligence augmentation systems with this quality. As a general rule, computer code tends to reflect the idiosyncrasies and biases of those doing the coding. So as we move toward higher levels of AI and its associated dangers, perhaps the best safeguard against these dangers is to enhance our actual intelligence and sensitivity as actual humans.

> *"The two biggest obstacles to human-level AI are endowing computers with common sense and endowing them with creativity."*

Current Technology Cannot Emulate Human Intelligence

Guia Marie Del Prado

In the following viewpoint, the author presents firsthand accounts of the various challenges within the field of AI. A consensus emerges that computers are quite good at performing narrow tasks like winning a game. However, when it comes to flexible thinking, adaptation, desire, and will, computers lag far behind. Further complicating matters is the fact that no one can really explain the essence of these uniquely human traits—we still do not truly know understand consciousness and intelligence. Thus, many believe that despite coming gains in computational power, the task of defining and replicating the human experience will remain elusive. Guia Marie Del Prado covers health, technology, and science at Tech Insider.

"Experts explain the biggest obstacles to creating human-like robots," Guia Marie Del Prado, Business Insider, March 9, 2016. Reprinted by permission.

As you read, consider the following questions:

1. Why do some believe that computers should approach learning as a baby might?
2. What makes endowing a computer with common sense and creativity so difficult?
3. In general, what kinds of tasks are computers good at? What are computers less able to do effectively, compared to humans?

Artificial intelligence (AI) became a scientific field almost 60 years ago. Ever since then, researchers have tried to achieve human-level smarts or better.

Yet even with recent feats of computational genius—for example, Google DeepMind beating a human player in the game Go—AI scientists say they still have a long road ahead.

Tech Insider spoke with AI researchers, computer scientists, and roboticists around the world about what it is going to take to build a machine that's able to think, work, and feel like a human.

Scroll down to see their lightly edited responses.

Bart Selman said computers need to learn how to understand the world like a human.

"The big obstacle, though it's not an obstacle because I think it will just take time, is the computer has to learn more about the way we see the world.

"It's very hard to understand the world from a human perspective. Intelligence relies on the way we view the world as humans, and the way we think about the world.

"Computers are just starting to be able to hear and starting to being able to see images. Those are tremendous improvements in the field in the last five years.

"We're doing that by having computers read millions of texts and pages from the web, by hooking them up to cameras and moving them around human environments."

Commentary from Bart Selman, a computer scientist at Cornell University.

This experience of the world will foster more intelligent AI, Peter Norvig says.

"AI needs to experience living in the world.

"We are very good at gathering data and developing algorithms to reason with that data. But that reasoning is only as good as the data, which, for the AI we have now, is one step removed from reality.

"Reasoning will be improved as we develop systems that continuously sense and interact with the world, as opposed to learning systems that passively observe information that others have chosen."

Commentary from Peter Norvig, director of research at Google.

To do that, Yoshua Bengio says computers should be trained to learn like children.

"Right now, all of the impressive progress we've made is mostly due to supervised learning, where we take advantage of large quantities of data that have already been annotated by humans.

"This supervised learning thing is not how humans learn.

"Before two years of age, a child understands the visual world through experiencing it, moving their head and looking around.

"There's no teacher that tells the child, 'in the image that's currently in your retina, there's a cat, and furthermore it's at this location' and for each pixel of the image say 'this is background and this is cat.' Humans are able to learn just by observation and experience with the world.

"In comparison to human learning, AI researchers are not doing that great."

Commentary from Yoshua Bengio, a computer scientist at University of Montreal.

Yann LeCun echoes the idea that computers need to be more like babies.

"The short answer is: we have no idea. That's why it's very difficult to make predictions as to when 'human-level AI' will come about.

"Right now, though, the main obstacle we face is how to get machines to learn in an unsupervised manner, like babies and animals do."

Commentary from Yann LeCun, director of Facebook Artificial Intelligence Research.

That includes learning a kind of common sense, says Ernest Davis.

"The lack of common sense reasoning is a major obstacle. There's large amounts of basic understanding of the world that we haven't been able to get programs to do.

"To a very large extent, AI programs work by avoiding the problem, work by getting around the understanding of language or understanding what the text means and what it says about the world. There are limits to that.

"Before we can get fully intelligent programs, those problems are going to have to be overcome. But we don't know how we ourselves understand the world, mostly, so these traits are incredibly difficult to emulate in a program."

Commentary from Ernest Davis, computer scientist at New York University.

Murray Shanahan notes that computers also need to be more creative.

"The two biggest obstacles to human-level AI are endowing computers with common sense and endowing them with creativity.

"By endowing them with common sense, I mean giving computers the ability to understand the consequences of everyday actions—actions on physical things or social actions, things that you say or do with other people.

"By creativity, I don't mean the kind of thing that Mozart or Einstein could do, but the kind of thing that every child is capable of when they play.

"That kind of creativity is just being able to come up with completely new sorts of behavior and to explore them in an effective way, which children are amazing at. That's how they learn.

"We really don't know quite how to endow computers with those two capabilities yet."

Commentary from Murray Shanahan, a computer scientist at Imperial College.

Carlos Guestrin said computers need to be able to understand abstract concepts like humans do.
"Humans have developed what are called abstractions—we can think about, for example, cars generically without thinking about a specific type of car, but we can also quickly dig down to a specific car and to parts of cars. We can learn about those abstract notions and those specific notions very quickly through only a few examples.

"Today, it takes computers a lot of data, a lot of examples of cars, to learn what a car is. Then to generalize and represent different levels of abstractions or different levels of specificity is extremely difficult.

"That's one big gap between what a human can do, even a child can do, and what a computer can do."

Commentary from Carlos Guestrin, the CEO and cofounder of Dato, a company that builds artificially intelligent systems to analyze data.

The fundamental problem is that AI can only do what they're told to do, says Michael Littman.
"Some of the great successes lately have been things like deep learning—methods that take lots and lots of data and then are able to mimic human judgments about that data. Things like object recognition—where you show the computer a picture and

it can label that picture, 'oh that's a woman by the beach,' that kind of thing.

"What's missing from a lot of these systems at the moment is a notion of a will—a desire to do something in the world. It's just doing what it's told, which is to map inputs to outputs.

"There's not a lot of room for creativity there. The kinds of problems we are asking these systems to do are not really on a path towards a sentient system."

Commentary from Michael Littman, a computer scientist at Brown University

Matthew Taylor says computers just can't do as many things as humans can.

"Programs that think like humans are so far beyond where we are right now. I don't think the field even knows the right direction to in go to achieve that goal, let alone what the big roadblocks are.

"It would be really nice if we had artificial general intelligence but that's a long way away. Even winning Jeopardy, that's still a very constrained situation.

"That computer didn't need to know anything about how to walk or how to move, it didn't need to know that water is wet, or that people eat food—all this basic stuff that we take for granted.

"Computers have a ways to go before they can even use that kind of knowledge."

Commentary from Matthew Taylor, a computer scientist at Washington State University.

Toby Walsh says computers need to be more adaptable.

"We have some pretty good examples of superhuman performance, computers able to perform at levels which exceed those of humans.

"In the game of chess, answering questions on Jeopardy!— computers have clearly, demonstrably proved themselves able to perform at the level if not above the level of humans."

"But the thing that humans are just so wonderful at is our adaptability, our ability to work in new situations. If I parachute you into a new situation, you will very quickly adapt and work in that situation.

"Computers are still driven and very focused on what they've been told to do—they're very unadaptable at working.

"If you change the parameters, like 'don't play chess, play backgammon.' The Deep Blue chess-playing program is no good at backgammon. Getting the breadth of ability of humans is certainly going to be a big challenge."

Commentary from Toby Walsh, a professor in AI at the National Information and Communications Technology Australia.

Shimon Whiteson said we need to figure out how to get robots to move quickly between tasks.

"If we are talking about building a system that has intelligence which is at a comparable level to that of a human being, one bottleneck is computational power. The hardware just needs to get better. But this is a very transient obstacle because computers are getting faster all the time.

"It will only be a matter of years before we have much more powerful computers that can do things we can't even imagine today. When the computational power is here I think we have good algorithms for doing AI, good algorithms for learning.

"But there are some things we can't do well. Humans, for example, are really good at generalizing in different situations.

"You learn one task and can very quickly apply what you've learned to a different task, even if the relationship between the tasks is not that obvious. This is something that computers are really bad at that we don't have good algorithms for."

Commentary from Shimon Whiteson, an associate professor at the Informatics Institute at the University of Amsterdam.

Thomas Dietterich says we need to build computers that can do different things.

"When people talk about 'human-level AI' they typically mean 'human-breadth AI.'

"Adult humans can answer questions and solve problems across a wide range of activities—finance, sports, child rearing, collaboration, opening packages, planning trips, packing a car, and shopping for a vacuum cleaner.

"No AI system comes anywhere close to having this immense breadth of capabilities, particularly when it comes to combining vision, language, and physical manipulation.

"Additionally, we don't even know how to represent the knowledge and information that is needed for all of these different tasks.

"Hardly any AI research groups are studying this question. Instead, they are focused on improving computer performance on narrow tasks.

"It is easier to make progress and measure success on narrow tasks, whereas it is difficult to develop useful measures of general intelligence. We hardly know where to begin."

Commentary from Thomas Dietterich, the President of the Association for the Advancement of Artificial Intelligence.

To build a computer that can do all the different things a human can, Subbarao Kambhapati says two areas that have developed in isolation need to come together.
"There is great progress being made in understanding low level perception—being able to see the world, hear the world, touch the world, open doors—a very complicated, very technically challenging set of capabilities.

"We have also made progress at the top level—being able to reason about other people's minds, and then trying to anticipate their actions.

"But these pieces have been done separately, and bridging them is going to be a very important challenge.

"For example, when humans see a surveillance video, we start making a story up in their minds, that this guy is trying to do the following thing and this other guy is trying to do the following thing.

"That ability requires two different sorts of processing—one is low-level vision, and the other is higher-level reasoning about people's goals and intentions. They need to be combined."

Commentary from Subbarao Kambhapati, computer scientist at Arizona State University.

Lynne Parker says we don't have a single clue about how to build thinking, conscious machines.

"I don't have an answer for the obstacles in our way to building human-like robots, because we just don't know enough about how people reason. We haven't figured out the fundamental principles, so I don't think we know what the hurdles are.

"Maybe we need to find a way of representing and interconnecting facts, knowledge, and methods of reasoning—the whole structure of what intelligence looks like might be necessary to understand in order to achieve sentient reasoning in AI, but we don't even know what that looks like in the human brain.

"Whether or not we can achieve that without mimicking the human brain, I don't know. But there's something fundamental that we're not getting, in terms of how AI should be structured."

Commentary from Lynne Parker, the division director for the Information and Intelligent Systems Division at the National Science Foundation.

Particularly because we don't know how humans reason or create consciousness, according to Manuela Veloso.

"The obstacles are that we don't know much about how humans reason.

"We do know that humans can make a lot of decisions that are connected to functions. They can cross roads, they can pick up objects, they can construct things.

"We have to understand how people do it, but we also have to define the problems in a way that we can find algorithms to do them."

Commentary from Manuela Veloso, a computer scientist at Carnegie Mellon University.

Stuart Russell thinks we need to knock consciousness off its pedestal.

"I used to say that if you gave me a trillion dollars to build a sentient or conscious machine I would give it back. Because I could not honestly say I have any idea how it might work.

"Consciousness is a first person subjective experience. We don't have any scientific theory of any kind that could lead us to a detailed map of it.

"Even if we could simulate someone's brain in exquisite detail, there's nothing in any scientific theory that I'm aware of that can tell us that the operation of that particular physical system would generate a conscious experience.

"We don't have even the beginnings of a theory whose conclusion would be 'such and such a system is conscious.'"

Commentary from Stuart Russell, a computer scientist at the University of California, Berkeley.

Yoky Matsuoka says that it's not even clear that just adding more computational power will result in intelligence.

"One of the problems with AI is that it's very much a black box approach.

"Deep learning is a good example. Because it's such a black box, it's difficult for humans to comprehend everything that's going on inside the neural networks.

"To advance that, the only sort of knowledge we have is to say 'let's increase the number of neurons, number of connections, the computational power to increase the memory.'

"If we really build the number of neurons similar to the human brain and made all the right connections and started putting the same inputs in, are we really going to achieve human-level intelligence?

"We don't know. That's the problem."

Commentary from Yoky Matsuoka, former vice president of technology at Nest, a Google-owned company that makes smart thermostats.

On the other hand, Geoffrey Hinton says consciousness is besides the point.

"The biggest obstacle is the idea that there is some mysterious essence called 'consciousness' that is required to make things sentient.

"Consciousness is an old and very primitive attempt to explain what's special about a very complicated computational system—the human brain—by appealing to some unobserved essence.

"The concept is no more useful than the concept of 'oomph' for explaining what makes cars go.

"It's true that some cars have a lot more oomph than others, but that doesn't explain anything about how they work."

Commentary from Geoffrey Hinton, researcher at Google and computer scientist at the University of Toronto.

Samy Bengio says AI may not even go in the direction of an sentient, all-knowing robot.

Something like 'human intelligence,' it's not even clear AI research will evolve in that direction one day.

"Many pieces are still missing—in particular a better use and interaction of a long term memory and perception-based models. Models, like the Neural Turing Machine or Memory Networks, can achieve some of this, but it's only the beginning.

"We also need to be able to learn more with unlabeled or less labeled data, which is still an open research problem.

"We need to work more on continuous learning—the idea that we don't need to start training our models from scratch every time we have new data or algorithms to try. These are simply very difficult tasks that will certainly take a very long period of time to improve."

Commentary from Samy Bengio, researcher at Google.

For now, we should focus on improving what's possible, Sabine Hauert says.

The first challenge is actually understanding what sentient reasoning means. Nobody has a good definition of that. I personally believe that we're very far from anything that is deemed to be sentient.

"The second obstacle is the way we communicate about AI. There's a lot of hype and a lot of misconception around robotics and AI.

"A lot of it has to do with using words like 'sentient reasoning,' which is very far from anything that's there already. As a result of that, I think we're not talking about the right things.

"Instead of talking about sentient reasoning, I think we should be spending time thinking about the technologies that are much closer to happening.

"Trying to understand what their benefits are, what their impact is to society, what the legal and safety questions are."

Commentary from Sabine Hauert, a roboticist at Bristol University.

"If we're lucky, we might just end up building something that really understands us."

Researchers Should Focus On Emotionally Intelligent AI

Gideon Rosenblatt

In the following viewpoint, Gideon Rosenblatt discusses an area of research he believes is crucial for AI—artificial emotional intelligence. Unlike rational computer programs, artificial emotional intelligence is inspired by simple, organic structures that learn from their environment and "feel" emotions in an embodied manner. Although this field is young, technology firms are already interested in our emotions as part of a business model. Rosenblatt believes that artificial emotional intelligence can go further and decode our emotions even when they are not fully apparent to us. This could be a tremendous boon to human growth. Gideon Rosenblatt is a technologist with a background in business and social change.

As you read, consider the following questions:

1. Why does the author believe that emotional intelligence is essential to AI?
2. How are tech companies exploring emotional intelligence?
3. What are the author's hopes for the future of emotional intelligence research?

"Why Artificial Emotional Intelligence Really Matters," Gideon Rosenblatt, The Vital Edge, July 31, 2014. http://www.the-vital-edge.com/artificial-emotional-intelligence. Licensed under a CC BY 4.0 International.

The way that we understand one another has been finely tuned over millions of years, to the point where it's hard to believe anything could outperform humans when it comes to understanding humans. I'm convinced though, that within the next five to ten years, that belief will gradually disappear, as machines get better and better at making sense of our emotions.

This is the field of affective computing, or what I affectionately call, artificial emotional intelligence.

Why Emotional Intelligence Matters to Artificial Intelligence

The first signs of the shift to more emotionally intelligent software are already starting to appear on the market, and I'll touch on them in a moment. But first, I want to disclose a strong conviction: I believe *emotional* intelligence is absolutely essential to *artificial* intelligence. There are two reasons I believe this.

The first reason is that solving emotional intelligence is a more natural path to solving true machine thinking. There's still important work in more rules-based, rational approaches to artificial intelligence such as expert systems. But if you look at were the bulk of artificial intelligence research is today, it seems to be very roughly following the path that nature took when it first developed intelligence long, long ago.

Just look at the field of robotics and the increased interest in much simpler (and cheaper) designs that often draw inspiration from more primitive forms of life in nature. This is a more *embodied* approach to intelligence, and one that draw heavily on sensors as a way to embed robots in their environment to learn from it through physical feedback.

Beyond robotics, there is now also a much larger focus on pattern recognition and new approaches that look quite different from our original, more structured attempts at artificial intelligence. Look at the major investments that Google and other companies are making in Deep Learning and other cuts at machine learning. The more I dig into these approaches, the more I see analogies to primitive nervous systems, running pattern recognition processes on incoming sensory data.

If we are, in some loose way, following nature's path to developing intelligence, it's important to remember that our higher-level cognitive processing sits on top of a layer of emotion processing that is distributed throughout our bodies and in the more primitive centers of our brains. As we reach for true machine thinking, skipping this emotional layer might not only lead to undesirable consequences (machines without the the capacity to feel the difference between right and wrong, for example); it just plain might not be possible.

The second reason emotional intelligence is so important is that, for the foreseeable future at least, it is humans that will teach our artificial intelligence progeny what it needs to know in order to evolve. If our machines lack the capacity for understanding emotions, they will be severely handicapped in their ability to learn from us.

Why Emotional Intelligence Matters to Tech Companies

It's unlikely that we will see any shortage of interest in emotional intelligence from today's developers and users of artificial intelligence. Why? Because there will be a great deal of money in it.

Facebook's recent experiments in manipulating emotions in their stream seem ultimately to have been done out of concern that seeing negative emotions from other people on Facebook might reduce the amount of time that users were willing to spend on the service. That obviously has a huge impact on the company's earnings potential.

With all of the hullaballoo surrounding the Facebook controversy, few commentators have really focused on the limitations to the current generation of tools for doing this kinds of sentiment analysis. Most sentiment analysis tools today are text-based approaches that, at the most basic level, map words to sentiments. They tend not to deal well with sarcasm and other forms of human nuance, and work best in situations where is a large sampling of text to draw from, which makes them somewhat ill-suited to very short posts most people tend to make on social media.

I've no doubt that these text-based approaches will improve over time though. For companies like Facebook, Google, and Amazon, where user opinions are such an important aspect of their business model, there is just a lot of incentives to continue investing here.

Interestingly, it looks like we won't have to rely solely on text-based approaches to machine-based emotional intelligence for long. Affectiva, a startup with roots in the MIT Media Lab's Affective Computing group, has developed software that reads people's emotions through sophisticated facial recognition algorithms. The company is not alone in this space, but if they get it right, they could be sitting on a *huge* opportunity.

Clearly, there is a lot happening right now in the area of building more emotional intelligence into computing. Researchers at Microsoft are even experimenting with bras that will warn you when you are stress eating and clothing that will signal the emotional state of its wearer. All this work will no doubt continue because, regardless of whether we might actually want shirts that shimmer or flap when we're happy, there is big money in understanding how people actually feel about particular advertisements, political candidates, products and many other things.

Why Emotional Intelligence Really Matters

The real question that emerges from all this though, at least from my perspective, is how will all this artificial emotional intelligence work actually benefit the world? And here I will leave you with some surprising research out of USC that finds that people are much more willing to discuss their problems with virtual avatars than they are with real people. The key reasons for this stem from the program's superior abilities in building rapport (largely through empathetic listening with facial expressions and nodding) and because the test subjects felt that the avatar would not judge them (which a human might). There is great potential here, even if it might eventually represent a threat to professionals with backgrounds in counseling.

If we are lucky, we may just end up building something that isn't just about trying to understand one another's emotions so that we can more easily manipulate them. If we're lucky, we might just end up building something that really understands us. And for a variety of really deep reasons that I hope to detail in future posts, I believe that it's this understanding that may well be our most important legacy.

> "*The main advantage we have over future AIs is simply that we exist here, now, and can shape society to map out their rights and responsibilities before they arrive—while also building as many safeguards as we can against direct competition with them.*"

We Need to Determine What Defines a Person

Corin Faife

In the following viewpoint, Corin Faife examines the ethical, legal, and political questions that will arise as AI technology becomes more sophisticated. He uses the example of animals with humanlike intelligence and whether they should or should not enjoy certain legal rights. The same will be true of sophisticated AI, and it is up to experts now to define what constitutes a person and what rights to grant them once they become potentially more powerful than humans. Corin Faife is a journalist who writes about technology and urban development.

As you read, consider the following questions:

1. What animal has more genetic similarities with humans than gorillas?
2. What main advantage do humans have over AI?
3. Why is it important to set clear ethical guidelines around AI research now?

The things that define something as someone—as a person—are complex, contested, and mutable. Thinking about the moral, legal, and philosophical arguments around who does and does not get to be a person is a crucial step as we move ever closer toward the birth of the first truly sentient machines, and the destruction of the most highly sentient, endangered animals.

What level of sophistication will artificial intelligences need to attain before we consider them people—and all the rights that entails? And at what point on the spectrum of intelligence will we be creating machines that are as smart, and as deserving of legal rights, as the sentient animals we're driving to extinction?

"The same arguments we're making now on behalf of chimpanzees are the same arguments that will be made when, and if, robots ever can attain consciousness," said Steve Wise, president of the Nonhuman Rights Project.

For years, NRP staff has mounted legal challenges on behalf of nonhuman animals, hoping to use legal, moral, and scientific arguments to change the status of high-order, nonhuman animals from "things" to "persons."

The chimpanzee shares about 99 percent of its DNA with humans—which means that, surprisingly, they have more genetic similarities with us than they do with gorillas. Like humans, chimpanzees have only a small number of offspring, with females usually giving birth once every five years of sexual maturity, and on average rearing only three children to full adulthood. In social groups they perform cooperative problem solving, teach and learn from one another, and use rudimentary tools; mentally they have at least some concept of self, an IQ comparable to a toddler, and can actually outperform humans on certain cognitive tasks.

Chimpanzees also display friendship, joy, love, fear, and sadness through body language clearly readable by human emotional standards. When exposed to stress and trauma, they have behavioral disturbances that, in some cases, meet DSM-IV criteria for depression and PTSD.

So, then, here is a question that's all but unavoidable in a discussion of animal personhood: Is it all right that we've collectively decided such a creature does not deserve any of the same legal rights—not even a small subset of the rights—that a human being has?

"For many centuries, the essential distinction between entities has been that of those who are things—who lack the capacity for any legal rights—and those who are persons, who have the capacity for one or more legal rights," Wise said. "We've spent many years preparing a long-term, strategic litigation campaign … where we put forward arguments that elephants or chimpanzees or orcas ought to have legal rights, in fact ought to be legal persons, in terms of the sorts of values and principles which judges themselves hold."

In a case last year, one of their most high profile to date, lawyers from the Nonhuman Rights Project brought an argument to the New York City Supreme Court, which hinged on whether the writ of habeas corpus applied to two chimpanzees being held for use in medical experiments. The presiding judge ordered that the president of Stony Brook University, where the chimps were held, appear in court to argue against the case that they were being "unlawfully detained"—which by extension would imply that the chimps were legal persons with a right to due process. Although the judge later amended her order to remove the words "writ of habeas corpus," and clarified that she had not intended to suggest that chimps have legal person status, it was an important milestone nonetheless.

The reaction from the public around NRP initiatives, Wise noted, has been largely positive—with the biggest resistance often coming from judges who are sometimes affronted by the unusual nature of the ensuing litigation. Meanwhile, he said, in recent times it's becoming more common for artificial intelligence researchers to contact him after hearing about his work.

Nick Bostrom, philosophy professor at Oxford University and director of the Future of Humanity Institute, is well known for writing about issues surrounding the development of superintelligent AI. Rather than debating the point at which an AI might be considered sentient, his work assumes that this will certainly happen at some point in the future, and instead questions how we should act in the present with the knowledge that we will eventually live alongside artificial minds exponentially more powerful than our own.

Though Bostrom's work is often cited in terms of the potential dangers of AI, he's also interested both in the idea of whether we should assign rights to artificial intelligence, and how those rights would be qualitatively different than the type of rights a natural person requires.

"If you had something that was exactly equivalent to a human, except running on a computer—something like a human upload—then there are still many novel ethical issues that arise," Bostrom said. "For example, a human simulation might want to copy itself, but we would not want to allow it freedom to infinitely reproduce, or else it could theoretically expand to take up all available resources. So in a world in which this exists, we cannot have both reproductive freedom and a welfare state that guarantees a minimum standard of living for everybody, since the two are mutually incompatible."

The idea of digital reproduction would also bring up entirely new problems for political representation, Bostrom noted, as the idea of "one person, one vote" would clearly not be democratic in a constituency of self-replicating voters. (Maybe in the future digital beings might have "legal" and "illegal" status, in much the same way that humans who enter a country without government permission cannot vote, claim health insurance, etc.)

In order to enjoy the best quality of life, a human upload would probably demand that it live on a fast computer, that never be paused or restarted without consent—permissions which could, conceivably, be the kind of things that will one day be enshrined as legal rights for sentient artificial beings.

At the moment, these debates are wildly speculative. But as Bostrom argues in his book *Superintelligence*, the main advantage we have over future AIs is simply that we exist here, now, and can shape society to map out their rights and responsibilities before they arrive—while also building as many safeguards as we can against direct competition with them. From that perspective, perhaps it would be foolish to throw away our head start.

"When we first think of artificial intelligence, our mind often goes to popular culture, science fiction, and the idea of an android—something like Data from *Star Trek*," said Max Daniel, co-executive director of Sentience Politics, a think tank producing policy on topics linked to morality and the reduction of suffering across all sentient beings.

"This is a being that can talk, and is in many ways similar to a human: It can communicate with us, complain if we mistreat it, and so on. But what is perhaps much more realistic to assume—and this is a concern that the German philosopher Thomas Metzinger has raised—is that the first digital beings would be much more limited in their abilities, in fact much closer to nonhuman animals than humans, and so could not properly signal to us whether they were suffering."

Because of this, Sentience Politics is advocating for a clear set of ethical guidelines around research on artificial intelligence, including putting careful controls in place to avoid a situation in which a sentient being is unknowingly created as part of a machine learning project. As part of this initiative, Daniel mentioned the importance of implementing an "excluded middle" policy, first articulated in a philosophy paper by two researchers at UC Riverside, Eric Schwitzgebel and Mara Garza. Essentially, the excluded middle policy states that we should only create artificial intelligences whose status is completely clear: They should be either low-order machines with no approximation of sentience, or high-order beings that we recognize as deserving of moral consideration. Anything in the ambiguous middle ground should be avoided to cause suffering.

Which raises the question: How do we differentiate between an artificial intelligence which learns to respond as if it is thinking and feeling, and one which is genuinely able to think and feel? What standard of proof would we ask for?

Provided we accept that it will one day be possible to create machines which experience some level of sentience, then giving them the right to ethical treatment seems uncontroversial. But what about rights that go beyond the scope of avoiding suffering and into the domain of personal fulfillment—the right not just to a life, but to one that includes liberty and the pursuit of happiness?

Before we continue any further, we need to step back for a minute to look again at how we define a "person."

From a legal standpoint human, human beings are natural persons capable of holding legal rights and obligations. However, many present legal systems—like that of the United States—permit the existence of other types of legal persons, which are not flesh-and-blood entities but may nonetheless be granted personhood rights.

Take, for example, corporate personhood, where the legal entity of a corporation—and not just the human beings which comprise it—can own property in its own name or be sued in a court of law. Sovereign states also exist as persons under international law, and in certain exceptional cases other natural entities can also be persons, such as in New Zealand where the Whanganui River was granted personhood after campaigning by indigenous activists.

"Personhood is a legal status for which sentience is neither a necessary nor a sufficient condition," said Michael Dorf, professor of law at Cornell and author of a recent book onabortion and animal rights. "It's not a necessary condition, because as a matter of law artificial entities like corporations can have personhood;

and it's not a sufficient condition because sentient animals, even those with advanced capabilities, lack personhood."

Additionally, Dorf said there's a tendency to think that personhood is an all-or-nothing position with regard to rights, but this is not necessarily the case. "It's actually possible to have rights and responsibilities à la carte: For example, infants are persons before the law but lack some of the rights an responsibilities that competent adult persons have—such as they can't vote, but then conversely can't be responsible for criminal acts."

So a legal person need not have the full set of rights of a natural person—and though it's tempting to claim self-evidence that all human beings have natural rights, as the Founding Fathers did, historically there was nothing certain or inviolable about the fact that all human beings should have full personhood.

From start to finish, the trans-Atlantic slave trade accounted for the kidnapping of 12.5 million Africans from Africa. Of these, an estimated 450,000 Africans were taken to the United States; in 1860, during the last recorded census before abolition in 1865, the number of African-Americans considered to be the legally owned property of another person totaled just short of four million.

The first Africans were brought to the Virginia plantations in 1609, but it took 50 years for the institution of slavery, and the status of slaves, to be legally codified. Since the British common law used at the time gave protections for persons that would have been incompatible with the brutal punishment slave masters administered, the 1669 Act About the Casual Killing of Slaves clarified that causing the death of a slave should not result in prosecution for murder, since it was effectively no more than the willful destruction of one's own property.

The fact that ownership and sanctioned murder of another human being was a foundation of American history should show us just how personhood is a concept that has so often been defined in the interests of dominant power groups. The history of the feminist movement likewise shows the struggle, hundreds of years long, for women to enjoy the same legal rights as men. Lest we forget, until roughly 150 years ago, married women had no legal right to own property. There are still almost 1.5 million Americans alive today who were born before the 19th Amendment guaranteed women the right to vote.

Personhood, then, is by no means a fixed category; but in the present day we tend to think of it as something that is innate in all humans, without needing a great deal of justification. In trying to evaluate the nature of our shared humanity, arguments on the basis of intelligence—the capacity to think—are quickly dismissed, since we know that there is huge variation within our species, and the suggestion that someone with a low IQ is less human is abhorrent. More often we veer toward a description based on sentience: the capacity to feel, particularly in a complex, emotional way.

Fully describing the nature of sentience among humans is hard enough—interrogating the nature of "the human condition" has been a staple of philosophical thought from time immemorial and shows no signs of being exhausted as a topic. So how do we begin to assess the nature of self, being, and sentience of minds which are artificially created? When will we reach a point that we perceive inorganic beings as possessing the capacity to feel?

For a long time the gold standard of artificial intelligence was the Turing Test, in which success or failure was defined by a computer's ability to talk with a human partner in such a way that the human was unable to identify it as a machine. But today, when we regularly converse with phones so smart they've even fooled students of artificial intelligence, it has become ever more apparent that mimicking language is not the same as thought.

But the central point to consider in discussing robotic sentience is not the sophistication of any system that we have currently built; it is that we have the ability to build systems which are able to learn. Many applications of artificial intelligence we encounter online, from chatbots to image tagging, employ artificial neural networks, a form of machine learning inspired by the design of biological nervous systems.

Given a large enough dataset and enough time to learn, neural networks are able to develop models which will allow them to carry out complex tasks with uncanny accuracy—such as recognizing faces, transcribing speech to text, or writing plays in iambic pentameter—without having been specifically programmed to do so. It's perfectly conceivable that as processing power increases and the range of available data on human behavior grows, neural networks will be created that are able to form some approximation of what it is to be human, and to communicate their own hopes and fears in a human-like way.

The law, as history attests, should not be set in stone. Besides being a collection of rules to help us govern ourselves, law represents a repository of knowledge about how the world works, and how we as a society should respond to issues around which there may be dispute. In this sense, the process of creating new laws, and specifically of allocating new rights to sentient beings which previously had none, can be seen as a process of increasing the level of compassion embodied in our social institutions.

We don't necessarily need to exhaust every argument for and against giving certain animals personhood to conclude that they are deserving of the benefit of the doubt; there is no downside here to being overly generous with our compassion. Likewise, though the debate on rights for artificially sentient beings may seem abstract and theoretical at present, we don't lose out by trying to map the route of least harm ahead of time, especially given the rate of technological change in this field.

In a book set out as a manual for living with conviction in challenging times, the political activist Paul Rogat Loeb wrote: "We become more human only in the company of other humans beings." As an addendum, maybe a conviction to act morally with regard to all beings—especially those that differ greatly from us—is ultimately something that makes us the most human of all.

> *"We need to recognize what it means for exponential technological change to be entering the labor market space for nonroutine jobs for the first time ever. Machines that can learn mean nothing humans do as a job is uniquely safe anymore."*

AI Will Take More Jobs from Humans

Scott Santens

In the following viewpoint, Scott Santens states that AI technology is now expanding at an exponential rate and much more quickly than we could have imagined. Technology has already taken jobs from humans and it will continue to do so as AI is developed to perform tasks once relegated to humans. For this reason, Santens argues, it is crucial that humans not rely on employment for their primary income. A universal basic income will allow humans to thrive while letting AI do the basic work. Scott Santens writes about current issues, such as society and basic income, for the Atlantic, Forbes, *and the* Huffington Post, *to name a few. He is the author of* Robonomics: Avoiding Technology-Based Job Loss.

"Deep Learning Is Going to Teach Us All the Lesson of Our Lives: Jobs Are for Machines," Scott Santens, Medium, March 16, 2016. https://medium.com/basic-income /deep-learning-is-going-to-teach-us-all-the-lesson-of-our-lives-jobs-are-for-machines -7c6442e37a49#.xb4xaqnwu. Licensed under CC BY-SA 4.0.

As you read, consider the following questions:

1. At what game did an AI beat Lee Se-dol?
2. What four categories does the author divide all work into?
3. What is the name of the AI personal assistant that will soon be doing much of our work?

O n December 2nd, 1942, a team of scientists led by Enrico Fermi came back from lunch and watched as humanity created the first self-sustaining nuclear reaction inside a pile of bricks and wood underneath a football field at the University of Chicago. Known to history as Chicago Pile-1, it was celebrated in silence with a single bottle of Chianti, for those who were there understood exactly what it meant for humankind, without any need for words.

Now, something new has occurred that, again, quietly changed the world forever. Like a whispered word in a foreign language, it was quiet in that you may have heard it, but its full meaning may not have been comprehended. However, it's vital we understand this new language, and what it's increasingly telling us, for the ramifications are set to alter everything we take for granted about the way our globalized economy functions, and the ways in which we as humans exist within it.

The language is a new class of machine learning known as deep learning, and the "whispered word" was a computer's use of it to seemingly out of nowhere defeat three-time European Go champion Fan Hui, not once but five times in a row without defeat. Many who read this news, considered that as impressive, but in no way comparable to a match against Lee Se-dol instead, who many consider to be one of the world's best living Go players, if not the best. Imagining such a grand duel of man versus machine, China's top Go player predicted that Lee would not lose a single game, and Lee himself confidently expected to possibly lose one at the most.

What actually ended up happening when they faced off? Lee went on to lose all but one of their match's five games. An AI named AlphaGo is now a better Go player than any human and has been granted the "divine" rank of 9 dan. In other words, its level of play borders on godlike. Go has officially fallen to machine, just as Jeopardy did before it to Watson, and chess before that to Deep Blue.

So, what is Go? Very simply, think of Go as Super Ultra Mega Chess. This may still sound like a small accomplishment, another feather in the cap of machines as they continue to prove themselves superior in the fun games we play, but it is no small accomplishment, and what's happening is no game.

AlphaGo's historic victory is a clear signal that we've gone from linear to parabolic. Advances in technology are now so visibly exponential in nature that we can expect to see a lot more milestones being crossed long before we would otherwise expect. These exponential advances, most notably in forms of artificial intelligence limited to specific tasks, we are entirely unprepared for as long as we continue to insist upon employment as our primary source of income.

[...]

Routine Work

All work can be divided into four types: routine and nonroutine, cognitive and manual. Routine work is the same stuff day in and day out, while nonroutine work varies. Within these two varieties, is the work that requires mostly our brains (cognitive) and the work that requires mostly our bodies (manual). Where once all four types saw growth, the stuff that is routine stagnated back in 1990. This happened because routine labor is easiest for technology to shoulder. Rules can be written for work that doesn't change, and that work can be better handled by machines.

Distressingly, it's exactly routine work that once formed the basis of the American middle class. It's routine manual work that Henry Ford transformed by paying people middle class wages to perform, and it's routine cognitive work that once filled US office spaces. Such jobs are now increasingly unavailable, leaving only

AI and Word Processing

Lately I've been thinking about the idea of planting human intelligence in a computer. If you had asked me about it ten years ago I would have said it'll never happen, but now I'm not so sure.

First, some kind of thinking is already in computers, almost invisibly. Here's an example. I type a lot of text into the browser, Chrome, and it's talking back to the Google servers and is constantly evaluating what I type.

Over time it gets better at showing stuff that needs correcting. It started with spelling errors. Now it understands proper names and it can highlight some bad grammar.

[...]

So this is good. I like it when my computers make my work smarter, automatically without me having to do anything. But I'm not sure this is thinking. It's a lot like data processing, something computers have been doing since the beginning.

The tough question is can we make computers think like a human and if we can should we want to? Much of what humans act on is unconscious emotion, not thought, based on how things feel. Should we teach computers to do that? Is that what we had in mind when we talk about computers thinking?

Pop out and look at the big picture. What's been accomplished with human thought? Where did all this thinking lead us to? An over-populated unsustainable civilization. More thinking like that? I hope not!

I'd like to know what people working on machine intelligence plan to have their computers think about and if they're really trying to get them to think like humans.

"Should Machines Think Like Humans?" Dave Winer, January 12, 2015.

two kinds of jobs with rosy outlooks: jobs that require so little thought, we pay people little to do them, and jobs that require so much thought, we pay people well to do them.

If we can now imagine our economy as a plane with four engines, where it can still fly on only two of them as long as they both keep roaring, we can avoid concerning ourselves with crashing. But what happens when our two remaining engines also fail? That's what the advancing fields of robotics and AI represent to those final two engines, because for the first time, we are successfully teaching machines to learn.

Neural Networks

I'm a writer at heart, but my educational background happens to be in psychology and physics. I'm fascinated by both of them so my undergraduate focus ended up being in the physics of the human brain, otherwise known as cognitive neuroscience. I think once you start to look into how the human brain works, how our mass of interconnected neurons somehow results in what we describe as the mind, everything changes. At least it did for me.

As a quick primer in the way our brains function, they're a giant network of interconnected cells. Some of these connections are short, and some are long. Some cells are only connected to one other, and some are connected to many. Electrical signals then pass through these connections, at various rates, and subsequent neural firings happen in turn. It's all kind of like falling dominoes, but far faster, larger, and more complex. The result amazingly is us, and what we've been learning about how we work, we've now begun applying to the way machines work.

One of these applications is the creation of deep neural networks—kind of like pared-down virtual brains. They provide an avenue to machine learning that's made incredible leaps that were previously thought to be much further down the road, if even possible at all. How? It's not just the obvious growing capability of our computers and our expanding knowledge in the neurosciences, but the vastly growing expanse of our collective data, aka big data.

Big Data

Big data isn't just some buzzword. It's information, and when it comes to information, we're creating more and more of it every day. In fact we're creating so much that a 2013 report by SINTEF estimated that 90% of all information in the world had been created in the prior two years. This incredible rate of data creation is even doubling every 1.5 years thanks to the Internet, where in 2015 every minute we were liking 4.2 million things on Facebook, uploading 300 hours of video to YouTube, and sending 350,000 tweets. Everything we do is generating data like never before, and lots of data is exactly what machines need in order to learn to learn. Why?

Imagine programming a computer to recognize a chair. You'd need to enter a ton of instructions, and the result would still be a program detecting chairs that aren't, and not detecting chairs that are. So how did we learn to detect chairs? Our parents pointed at a chair and said, "chair." Then we thought we had that whole chair thing all figured out, so we pointed at a table and said "chair", which is when our parents told us that was "table." This is called reinforcement learning. The label "chair" gets connected to every chair we see, such that certain neural pathways are weighted and others aren't. For "chair" to fire in our brains, what we perceive has to be close enough to our previous chair encounters. Essentially, our lives are big data filtered through our brains.

Deep Learning

The power of deep learning is that it's a way of using massive amounts of data to get machines to operate more like we do without giving them explicit instructions. Instead of describing "chairness" to a computer, we instead just plug it into the Internet and feed it millions of pictures of chairs. It can then have a general idea of "chairness." Next we test it with even more images. Where it's wrong, we correct it, which further improves its "chairness" detection. Repetition of this process results in a computer that knows what a chair is when it sees it, for the most part as well as we can. The important difference though is that unlike us, it can then sort through millions of images within a matter of seconds.

This combination of deep learning and big data has resulted in astounding accomplishments just in the past year. Aside from the incredible accomplishment of AlphaGo, Google's DeepMind AI learned how to read and comprehend what it read through hundreds of thousands of annotated news articles. DeepMind also taught itself to play dozens of Atari 2600 video games better than humans, just by looking at the screen and its score, and playing games repeatedly. An AI named Giraffe taught itself how to play chess in a similar manner using a dataset of 175 million chess positions, attaining International Master level status in just 72 hours by repeatedly playing itself. In 2015, an AI even passed a visual Turing test by learning to learn in a way that enabled it to be shown an unknown character in a fictional alphabet, then instantly reproduce that letter in a way that was entirely indistinguishable from a human given the same task. These are all major milestones in AI.

However, despite all these milestones, when asked to estimate when a computer would defeat a prominent Go player, the answer even just months prior to the announcement by Google of AlphaGo's victory, was by experts essentially, "Maybe in another ten years." A decade was considered a fair guess because Go is a game so complex I'll just let Ken Jennings of Jeopardy fame, another former champion human defeated by AI, describe it:

> Go is famously a more complex game than chess, with its larger board, longer games, and many more pieces. Google's DeepMind artificial intelligence team likes to say that there are more possible Go boards than atoms in the known universe, but that vastly understates the computational problem. There are about 10^{170} board positions in Go, and only 10^{80} atoms in the universe. That means that if there were as many parallel universes as there are atoms in our universe (!), then the total number of atoms in all those universes combined would be close to the possibilities on a single Go board.

Such confounding complexity makes impossible any brute-force approach to scan every possible move to determine the next best move. But deep neural networks get around that barrier in the same way our own minds do, by learning to estimate what feels like the best move. We do this through observation and practice, and so did AlphaGo, by analyzing millions of professional games and playing itself millions of times. So the answer to when the game of Go would fall to machines wasn't even close to ten years. The correct answer ended up being, "Any time now."

Nonroutine Automation

Any time now. That's the new go-to response in the 21st century for any question involving something new machines can do better than humans, and we need to try to wrap our heads around it.

We need to recognize what it means for exponential technological change to be entering the labor market space for nonroutine jobs for the first time ever. Machines that can learn mean nothing humans do as a job is uniquely safe anymore. From hamburgers to healthcare, machines can be created to successfully perform such tasks with no need or less need for humans, and at lower costs than humans.

Amelia is just one AI out there currently being beta-tested in companies right now. Created by IPsoft over the past 16 years, she's learned how to perform the work of call center employees. She can learn in seconds what takes us months, and she can do it in 20 languages. Because she's able to learn, she's able to do more over time. In one company putting her through the paces, she successfully handled one of every ten calls in the first week, and by the end of the second month, she could resolve six of ten calls. Because of this, it's been estimated that she can put 250 million people out of a job, worldwide.

Viv is an AI coming soon from the creators of Siri who'll be our own personal assistant. She'll perform tasks online for us, and even function as a Facebook News Feed on steroids by suggesting we consume the media she'll know we'll like best. In doing all of this for us, we'll see far fewer ads, and that means the entire advertising industry—that industry the entire Internet is built upon—stands to be hugely disrupted.

A world with Amelia and Viv—and the countless other AI counterparts coming online soon—in combination with robots like Boston Dynamics' next generation Atlas portends, is a world where machines can do all four types of jobs and that means serious societal reconsiderations. If a machine can do a job instead of a human, should any human be forced at the threat of destitution to perform that job? Should income itself remain coupled to employment, such that having a job is the only way to obtain income, when jobs for many are entirely unobtainable? If machines are performing an increasing percentage of our jobs for us, and not getting paid to do them, where does that money go instead? And what does it no longer buy? Is it even possible that many of the jobs we're creating don't need to exist at all, and only do because of the incomes they provide? These are questions we need to start asking, and fast.

Decoupling Income From Work

Fortunately, people are beginning to ask these questions, and there's an answer that's building up momentum. The idea is to put machines to work for us, but empower ourselves to seek out the forms of remaining work we as humans find most valuable, by simply providing everyone a monthly paycheck independent of work. This paycheck would be granted to all citizens unconditionally, and its name is universal basic income. By adopting UBI, aside from immunizing against the negative effects of automation, we'd also be decreasing the risks inherent in entrepreneurship, and the sizes of bureaucracies necessary to boost incomes. It's for these reasons, it has cross-partisan support, and is even now in the beginning stages of possible implementation in countries like Switzerland, Finland, the Netherlands, and Canada.

The future is a place of accelerating changes. It seems unwise to continue looking at the future as if it were the past, where just because new jobs have historically appeared, they always will. The WEF started 2016 off by estimating the creation by 2020 of 2 million new jobs alongside the elimination of 7 million. That's a net loss, not a net gain of 5 million jobs. In a frequently cited paper, an Oxford study estimated the automation of about half of all existing jobs by 2033. Meanwhile self-driving vehicles, again thanks to machine learning, have the capability of drastically impacting all economies—especially the US economy as I wrote last year about automating truck driving—by eliminating millions of jobs within a short span of time.

And now even the White House, in a stunning report to Congress, has put the probability at 83 percent that a worker making less than $20 an hour in 2010 will eventually lose their job to a machine. Even workers making as much as $40 an hour face odds of 31 percent. To ignore odds like these is tantamount to our now laughable "duck and cover" strategies for avoiding nuclear blasts during the Cold War.

All of this is why it's those most knowledgeable in the AI field who are now actively sounding the alarm for basic income. During a panel discussion at the end of 2015 at Singularity University, prominent data scientist Jeremy Howard asked "Do you want half of people to starve because they literally can't add economic value, or not?" before going on to suggest, "If the answer is not, then the smartest way to distribute the wealth is by implementing a universal basic income."

AI pioneer Chris Eliasmith, director of the Centre for Theoretical Neuroscience, warned about the immediate impacts of AI on society in an interview with Futurism, "AI is already having a big impact on our economies… My suspicion is that more countries will have to follow Finland's lead in exploring basic income guarantees for people."

Moshe Vardi expressed the same sentiment after speaking at the 2016 annual meeting of the American Association for the Advancement of Science about the emergence of intelligent machines, "we need to rethink the very basic structure of our economic system… we may have to consider instituting a basic income guarantee."

Even Baidu's chief scientist and founder of Google's "Google Brain" deep learning project, Andrew Ng, during an onstage interview at this year's Deep Learning Summit, expressed the shared notion that basic income must be "seriously considered" by governments, citing "a high chance that AI will create massive labor displacement."

When those building the tools begin warning about the implications of their use, shouldn't those wishing to use those tools listen with the utmost attention, especially when it's the very livelihoods of millions of people at stake? If not then, what about when Nobel prize winning economists begin agreeing with them in increasing numbers?

No nation is yet ready for the changes ahead. High labor force non-participation leads to social instability, and a lack of consumers within consumer economies leads to economic instability. So let's ask ourselves, what's the purpose of the technologies we're creating? What's the purpose of a car that can drive for us, or artificial intelligence that can shoulder 60% of our workload? Is it to allow us to work more hours for even less pay? Or is it to enable us to choose how we work, and to decline any pay/hours we deem insufficient because we're already earning the incomes that machines aren't?

What's the big lesson to learn, in a century when machines can learn?

I offer it's that jobs are for machines, and life is for people.

"Supercomputers can make us superhuman. As machines explore the depths of digital data, humans will be freed to innovate far and wide."

Collaborating with AI Will Make Humans More Creative

Loni Stark

In the following viewpoint, Loni Stark reverses the familiar sinister narrative in which robots become our future overlords. Instead, Stark argues that humans in all industries can take advantage of the massive power computers bring to certain tasks, such as analyzing data. In fact, many industries such as fashion and online commerce are already harnessing these powers. Future humans will need to be savvy collaborators to reap maximum benefit from machine intelligence. Stark also notes that tasks requiring empathy will be better served by humans. So if machines do the number crunching, this will free people up to be more creative at work. Loni Stark is senior director of strategy and product marketing at Adobe.

"Why Machine-Learning Will Enhance, Not Replace, Human Creativity," Loni Stark, Adobe, May 13, 2016. This article first appeared on Adobe's Digital Marketing blog. Reprinted by permission.

As you read, consider the following questions:

1. Why does the author claim machine learning will free humans to be more creative?
2. What are some examples of this happening today?
3. How does the author envision the machine-human workplace of the future?

Machines are getting smarter. And pretty soon, they'll come for us.

That seems to be the story today, whether from Hollywood or in breathless articles in popular tech magazines about artificial intelligence and nanotechnology.

In a world where machines can learn, once humans push the "on" button, there's no stopping our robot overlords, right?

Not exactly.

When machines become more intelligent, humans are freed to become more creative. That opens doors to completely new possibilities.

At the most basic level, machines "learn" by using algorithms to analyze data and find patterns or predict outcomes. Machine-learning technologies use the results they obtain to adapt their algorithms and improve them over time—they learn.

Amazon's recommendations engine is a simple example.

If the merchant feeds you a buying suggestion that turns out to be way off the mark, it will alter its process in an attempt to feed you better recommendations next time.

Pinterest recently unveiled a machine-learning search tool based on image recognition. Users can click on anything within an image on the site—a lamp in the background of an apartment setup, for instance, or a driving cap worn by the subject in an image—and Pinterest searches its entire archive to offer up visually similar results.

Data frees-up minds, and fuels them for creativity

Billionaire tech visionary Peter Thiel has pointed out that while machines are very good at processing massive amounts of data, they still can't make thoughtful decisions or draw sensible conclusions.

Judgment is still solidly handled by humans.

That's why the emergence of machine learning is so exciting. Computers free us up to concentrate on more creative tasks.

Rather than fearing machines, we should look for ways to harness them so we can better innovate.

After all, people used to worry about ATMs taking jobs away from bank tellers.

But machines count, collect, and distribute money much better than humans do. And by automating cash withdrawals and check deposits, banks were able to reallocate labor toward more complex tasks, like loan originations and advisory services.

Machines can't empathize. But humans can. So by freeing up labor, ATMs helped banks—and even bank tellers—better service their customers.

Ultimately, no algorithm could replicate the essential emotional connections needed to help a customer take out a mortgage, start a college fund, or make sense of a deceased parent's finances.

The fashion industry is on the verge of a similar evolution.

Researchers at the University of Toronto just announced they've completed a program that uses algorithmic learning and computer vision to identify people's fashion mistakes. The program can figure out which outfits work and which don't—and make recommendations on how to upgrade a wardrobe.

The widespread adoption of this technology would free up fashion specialists to provide more personalized guidance to shoppers and employ brilliant seasonal campaigns.

A similar trend is emerging in medicine.

Already, machine learning is helping doctors make better diagnoses. Eventually, it could help identify high-risk patients and predict readmissions, thus enabling physicians to better tailor their treatment plans. That could reduce health care costs and improve patient outcomes.

If this all seems a little too Pollyannaish, consider your everyday online browsing habits. Just like Amazon recommends products you may be interested in, YouTube recommends videos you might want to watch—and LinkedIn offers up blog posts you might want to read. These sites offer customized content you might never find on your own.

For creative types, these discoveries often inspire the development of even better content. A budding producer might discover a fun filming technique she had never thought of thanks to YouTube. A young entrepreneur might learn about a new method of office management on LinkedIn.

Embracing the future takes effort

While machines won't be our overlords, they will be our coworkers.

In just about every industry, people will have to embrace non-human collaborators. Aptly questioning and gathering input from sophisticated software—a healthy give and take between man and machine—will become the norm.

This is exciting.

Supercomputers can make us superhuman. As machines explore the depths of digital data, humans will be freed to innovate far and wide.

We're already seeing this with design-driven technology, a cross-section of art and science.

With machines handling the hard numbers, we'll have more time to embrace our human strengths of creativity and empathy. Marketers who embrace artificial intelligence have extra human capital to spend on artistic ideas and moving ads.

Thanks to machines, we're replacing the data-packed spreadsheet with the high-level marketing brainstorm session.

Albert Einstein famously, if apocryphally, used an algorithm to solve the problem of what to wear. His goal was to avoid wasting time and brainpower picking out clothes every morning. So each day, he wore one of several identical gray suits he'd purchased.

Of course, if Einstein had Netflix—or Bravo, if I'm being honest—perhaps he would have spent all the time he freed up by wearing the same outfit every day binge watching TV.

Algorithms and machine learning free us up to do other things with our time. But the onus is on us to take advantage of all those new opportunities.

Periodical and Internet Sources Bibliography

The following articles have been selected to supplement the diverse views presented in this chapter.

Dominic Basulto, "Humans Are the World's Best Pattern-Recognition Machines, But for How Long?" Big Think.

Suzanne Bouffard, "Teaching Computers to Think Like Humans," Fabbs Foundation, January 17, 2014.

Edge, various authors, "2015: What Do You Think About Machines That Think?" Edge, 2015.

David Gelernter, "Machines That Will Think and Feel," *Wall Street Journal*, March 18, 2016.

Satya Nadella, "The Partnership of the Future," Slate, June 28, 2016.

Scientific American, "Will Machines Ever Think Like Humans?" Scientific American, November 1, 2014.

Cadie Thompson, "The Big Reason Why Robots Are Starting to Act More Like Humans," *Business Insider*, July 12, 2015.

James Titcomb, "Should Humans Fear the Rise of the Machine?" *Telegraph*, September 1, 2015.

OPPOSING
VIEWPOINTS®
SERIES

CHAPTER 4

Is AI a Threat to the Human Race?

Chapter Preface

In addition to luminaries such as Bill Gates and Stephen Hawking, other notable thinkers and authors such as Nick Bostrom and James Barrat have each recently published books warning us about the possible perils of AI. Should we take these predictions seriously? Or is "existential concern" about robots misplaced and misguided?

Responses to this question typically splinter off in two directions. Some point out that speculation about future events that are relatively improbable, however disastrous if they might be if they were to come to pass, only distract us from more pressing questions of how machine intelligence is being used in problematic ways already. In addition, we might wonder why influential people are choosing to alert the public to such distant concerns over which they have little influence. Might this be a calculated tactic of misdirection? A play for publicity? Those of a more conspiratorial bend have entertained both possibilities. Regardless of ulterior motives, which of course must remain opaque, our purpose in this chapter is to evaluate critically the possible dangers and developments the age of AI could conceivably usher in, whilst sidestepping the more alarmist predictions in circulation on the internet and in print.

To begin, let us for a moment take seriously the possibility that human-level AI will materialize in our lifetimes. What dangers and risks would this emergent technology carry? According to James Barrat, AI would be a willful and egocentric beast. Like us, it would be partial to its own advancement and adverse to failure. Thus, if given the opportunity, AI would not think twice about hording resources such as energy and money. The classic problem with which theorists illustrate rogue robot intelligence is the imperative to maximize the production of paper clips. As the example goes, a robot would respond in a literal manner, using all available atoms in its purview to transform the entire earth into a giant supply of paper clips! Surely if technology advances far enough to create general artificial intelligence, it might also guard against such a bizarre example of technology gone awry. The obvious takeaway is that barring human administered failsafe measures, machine intelligence could be difficult to thwart if given a mandate and sufficient momentum.

One cannot help but see an anthropomorphic slant to such worst-case prognostications. In fact, human technological development has been subject to similar critiques of blind instrumentalism since the assumptions upon which Enlightenment rationality rests began to be questioned. While there is a chance that a manual override of AI could be difficult, the implications of the above scenario leans more toward a morass of bureaucracy. One can imagine claims of "the robots are in control" as simply another tool through which the ruling class abnegates social responsibility. Nowhere is this danger clearer than in the military. If we cede our power over life and death to increasingly sophisticated drones and other killing machines, who will be accountable?

> *"In determining the overall level of intelligence of a being, then, the scope and interrelatedness of the relevant capacities, rather than just the level of the individual capacities, is relevant."*

We Must Prevent Threats from AI Now
CyberNole

In the following viewpoint, CyberNole editor-in-chief Nick Farrell interviews Marcela Herdova, professor of philosophy at Florida State University, to get her take on AI's impact on society. Herdova uses a philosopher's approach to contemplate the big questions brought on by the development of AI. While it's impossible to predict the future based on technology that hasn't been created yet, Herdova believes that experts should consider AI's potential effects on society as they invent increasingly sophisticated technology. CyberNole is the premiere technology and science news journal of Florida State University.

As you read, consider the following questions:

1. Does the professor being interviewed believe AI could surpass human general intelligence?
2. Rather than contemplating AI rights, what word does the interview subject use?
3. In the series *Red Dwarf*, what did humans do to reduce the threat posed by robots?

"Artificial Intelligence: Tool for the Future, or Man's Last Invention?" Cybernole.net, April 2, 2015. http://cybernole.weebly.com/archive/artificial-intelligence-tool-for-the-future-or-mans-las-invention. Licensed under CC BY 4.0 International.

The rapid rise of computers and artificial intelligence over the last decade has been unparalleled by any technology in history. As we move forward, it is vital that we think about not only how fast we are moving forward, but also what lies at the end of the direction we are heading in.

Over the past month many industrialists and great thinkers such as Bill Gates, Elon Musk and more, have spoken of the danger in creating artificial intelligence that we cannot control, or that will someday control us.

Cybernole spoke with FSU philosophy professor Marcela Herdova to get her opinion on the matter.

CyberNole: At what point can you say that artificial intelligence is equal to human intelligence?

Marcela: Human intelligence is often broken down into sets of different (but likely highly interrelated) skills. That is, we have intelligence-related capabilities of different kinds. For example, some aspects of emotional intelligence, such as being able to recognize and appropriately respond to a range of emotions, are quite different from those skills which are involved in calculating one's next chess move, learning a foreign language, or working out a complicated equation.

It may be more helpful, then, to narrow down the question and sharpen our focus on individual facets of human intelligence when comparing it to artificial intelligence. For at least some sets of skills, we have already created AIs that have skills which are comparable to and beyond the skills of humans. Chess computers now routinely defeat even grandmasters at chess. This is, in part, because these computers are capable of making billions of calculations per second—something far beyond any human's capacities.

Still, even if we have created AI that surpasses human capabilities in some sense, it's not obvious that any kind of current artificial intelligence is comparable to or beyond human intelligence. One remarkable thing about intelligence, as we understand it, is its diversity and adaptability. Humans are excellent at turning their

Stephen Hawking's Warnings

Prof Stephen Hawking, one of Britain's pre-eminent scientists, has said that efforts to create thinking machines pose a threat to our very existence.

He told the BBC: "The development of full artificial intelligence could spell the end of the human race."

His warning came in response to a question about a revamp of the technology he uses to communicate, which involves a basic form of AI.

But others are less gloomy about AI's prospects.

The theoretical physicist, who has the motor neurone disease amyotrophic lateral sclerosis (ALS), is using a new system developed by Intel to speak.

Machine learning experts from the British company Swiftkey were also involved in its creation. Their technology, already employed as a smartphone keyboard app, learns how the professor thinks and suggests the words he might want to use next.

Prof Hawking says the primitive forms of artificial intelligence developed so far have already proved very useful, but he fears the consequences of creating something that can match or surpass humans.

"It would take off on its own, and re-design itself at an ever increasing rate," he said.

"Humans, who are limited by slow biological evolution, couldn't compete, and would be superseded."

[...]

In his BBC interview, Prof Hawking also talks of the benefits and dangers of the internet.

He quotes the director of GCHQ's warning about the net becoming the command centre for terrorists: "More must be done by the internet companies to counter the threat, but the difficulty is to do this without sacrificing freedom and privacy."

He has, however, been an enthusiastic early adopter of all kinds of communication technologies and is looking forward to being able to write much faster with his new system.

"Stephen Hawking Warns Artificial Intelligence Could End Mankind," Rory Cellan-Jones, BBC News, December 2, 2014.

minds to multiple areas, and conjuring up creative and ingenious ideas to solve problems. While we may not be able to make calculations as fast as computers, we are able both to find solutions in a more creative manner (without simply considering billions of possible chess moves, for example) and to turn our capabilities to an indefinite and wide range of topics. In determining the overall level of intelligence of a being, then, the scope and interrelatedness of the relevant capacities, rather than just the level of the individual capacities, is relevant.

This said, AI is catching up with us. There are computers that compose classical music, showing a level of creativity that most of us would not attribute to a computer. Computers show signs of learning, understanding and creativity. If researchers in AI find ways to enhance such capacities, and develop AI with a general intelligence (instead of an intelligence that is highly specialized), then I see no reason why AI could not surpass human intelligence.

Experts predict that this type of computer will exist in the next 30 years. What implications will this have for mankind?

Marcela: That's really difficult to say. Karl Popper famously elaborated on why we cannot understand or foresee the impact of various scientific discoveries before we actually make them: since we do not have enough knowledge about the nature of such discoveries, we cannot effectively consider what kind of impact they will have, especially if these discoveries might lead to a significant revision of the current body of knowledge. Similar considerations can also be applied with regards to the development of AI which would surpass human intelligence. From our standpoint today, we are not in a position to work out what kind of impact these beings or machines with capacities greater than ours would have—precisely because they would be more intelligent than us! We cannot make predictions about the consequences of creating AI more intelligent than humans because, to be able to do so, we would need to possess the level of intelligence this advanced AI is supposed to have. I am thus pessimistic at our prospects for predicting what might happen should AI surpass in intelligence. Others are pessimistic in another way: they worry that once AI surpass us, the human race will be threatened with extinction.

At what point does artificial intelligence deserve to have rights? Should they be the same as a person's rights?

Marcela: Some people will argue that rights are essentially human—they arise within a community of people and as such can be applied to humans only. On this basis, some will argue that non-human animals do not have rights, and, by extension, AIs are not the right candidates for having rights either. Personally, I do not find this approach very plausible. What might be more helpful is to think about what beings have "interests". If there is a being that has, for example, an interest in survival, not suffering, etc., then we should perhaps give such interests some—perhaps even equal—consideration in our moral thinking. Indeed, a capacity to have interests at all plausibly grounds having moral rights.

This thinking is similar to Peter Singer's very influential claim that non-human animals should be given equal consideration due to their interests in not suffering. If a being that is not a member of our species has interests parallel to human interests, those deserve equal consideration. If we create AI which has the capacity for suffering, which is arguably both necessary and sufficient for having any interests at all, this is a weighty consideration in favor of this AI's having rights.

As for the question of whether such a being should have rights which are similar to a person's rights, this will depend on the specifics of this AI. If it has not only the capacity to suffer, but also to value its continued existence, and pursuit of fulfillment, I do not see why it should not have at least the same basic rights that we usually afford to members of our species. What other rights this being might have will further depend on its abilities and interests.

What do you think of the threat of artificial intelligence becoming too powerful for humans to control?

Marcela: That kind of threat seems to be at least conceivable. But whether conceivability is a good guide to possibility is one of the big and challenging debates in philosophy. So even if such a threat is conceivable, it is far from obvious that this is likely to happen, or even that it could happen.

Some people do, however, seem to think that AI can pose a significant threat to us. For example, in a recent interview, Professor Stephen Hawking expressed concerns about how artificial intelligence could end mankind. One of the main worries Hawking has is that if we create AI that matches or surpasses human intelligence, then AI would able to re-design and improve itself at a rapid rate (this is the idea behind the so-called "technological singularity"). Should that happen, then humans might fall behind and be superseded by AI given that the evolution of our species is, comparatively, rather slow.

I think with regards to preventing such a threat, a lot depends on whether or how successfully we can create artificial intelligence that follows something akin to the three laws of robotics put forward by Isaac Asimov. Essentially, these three laws together make it so that any artificial intelligence should not harm any human being or allow for such harm—not even when given orders to do so (otherwise any other orders should be straightforwardly followed) or protecting itself. I presume that if we can create artificial intelligence which follows these rules, and sufficiently protect these from being tampered with, any such threats would be greatly reduced.

Another possibility stems from a suggestion made in the television series *Red Dwarf*, and expanded on in the second novel based on the series. In this novel, *Better Than Life*, AI are kept from rebelling and violently killing us in a rather inventive manner.

> Back in the twenty-first century, as robotic life became more and more sophisticated, it was generally accepted that something was needed to keep the droids in check. For the most part they were stronger, and often more intelligent, than human beings:

why should they submit to second-class status, to a lifetime of drudgery and service?

Many of them didn't.

Many of them rebelled.

Then it occurred to a bright young systems analyst at Android International that the best way to keep the robots subdued was to give them religion.

Hallelujah!

The concept of Silicon Heaven was born.

A belief chip was implanted in the motherboard of every droid that now came off the production line.

Almost everything with a hint of artificial intelligence was programmed to believe that Silicon Heaven was the electronic afterlife—the final resting place for the souls of all electrical equipment.

The concept ran thus: if machines served their human masters with diligence and dedication, they would attain everlasting life in mechanical paradise when their components finally ran down. In Silicon Heaven, they would be reunited with their electrical loved ones. In Silicon Heaven, there would be no pain or suffering. It was a place where the computer never crashed, the laser printer never ran out of toner, and the photocopier never had a paper jam.

At last, they had solace. They were every bit as exploited as they'd always been, but now they believed there was some kind of justice at the end of it all.

Perhaps this suggestion deserves more serious attention than it has thus far received. But, then again, perhaps not.

> *"In this century, scientists will create machines with intelligence that equals and then surpasses our own. But before we share the planet with super-intelligent machines, we must develop a science for understanding them."*

Human-Level AI Cannot Easily Be Controlled

Erica R. Hendry

In the following interview with James Barrat, author of Our Final Invention, *Erica Hendry examines the minority viewpoint that intelligent machines will revolutionize life on Earth, and not necessarily in a way that takes human priorities into account. Barrat cites a few developments already pointing in this direction: private, profit-driven AI research, the inevitable weaponization of AI, and abuses of privacy by the NSA. He also disagrees with the optimistic transhumanism of Ray Kurzweil, believing instead that machine intelligence will pursue its own agenda. Controlling this agenda will be difficult, unless we begin now. Erica R. Hendry is the innovations reporter and producer for Smithsonian.com.*

"What Happens When Artificial Intelligence Turns on Us?" Erica R. Hendry, Smithsonian .com, January 21, 2014. Reprinted by permission.

As you read, consider the following questions:

1. What are some present-day examples of irresponsible AI use? Are these inherent problems with the technology or human decisions and failings?
2. According to Barrat, why is so little being done now to safeguard humans against AI?
3. How might AI be made safe? What is the author's prognosis on this?

Artificial intelligence has come a long way since R2-D2. These days, most millennials would be lost without smart GPS systems. Robots are already navigating battlefields, and drones may soon be delivering Amazon packages to our doorsteps.

Siri can solve complicated equations and tell you how to cook rice. She has even proven she can even respond to questions with a sense of humor.

But all of these advances depend on a user giving the A.I. direction. What would happen if GPS units decided they didn't want to go to the dry cleaners, or worse, Siri decided she could become smarter without you around?

These are just the tamest of outcomes James Barrat, an author and documentary filmmaker, forecasts in his new book, *Our Final Invention: Artificial Intelligence and the End of the Human Era.*

Before long, Barrat says, artificial intelligence—from Siri to drones and data mining systems—will stop looking to humans for upgrades and start seeking improvements on their own. And unlike the R2-D2s and HALs of science fiction, the A.I. of our future won't necessarily be friendly, he says: they could actually be what destroy us.

In a nutshell, can you explain your big idea?
In this century, scientists will create machines with intelligence that equals and then surpasses our own. But before we share the planet with super-intelligent machines, we must develop a science

for understanding them. Otherwise, they'll take control. And no, this isn't science fiction.

Scientists have already created machines that are better than humans at chess, *Jeopardy!*, navigation, data mining, search, theorem proving and countless other tasks. Eventually, machines will be created that are better than humans at A.I. research

At that point, they will be able to improve their own capabilities very quickly. These self-improving machines will pursue the goals they're created with, whether they be space exploration, playing chess or picking stocks. To succeed they'll seek and expend resources, be it energy or money. They'll seek to avoid the failure modes, like being switched off or unplugged. In short, they'll develop drives, including self-protection and resource acquisition—drives much like our own. They won't hesitate to beg, borrow, steal and worse to get what they need.

How did you get interested in this topic?

I'm a documentary filmmaker. In 2000, I interviewed inventor Ray Kurzweil, roboticist Rodney Brooks and sci-fi legend Arthur C. Clarke for a TLC film about the making of the novel and film, *2001: A Space Odyssey*. The interviews explored the idea of the Hal 9000, and malevolent computers. Kurzweil's books have portrayed the A.I. future as a rapturous "singularity," a period in which technological advances outpace humans' ability to understand them. Yet he anticipated only good things emerging from A.I. that is strong enough to match and then surpass human intelligence. He predicts that we'll be able to reprogram the cells of our bodies to defeat disease and aging. We'll develop super endurance with nanobots that deliver more oxygen than red blood cells. We'll supercharge our brains with computer implants so that we'll become superintelligent. And we'll port our brains to a more durable medium than our present "wetware" and live forever if we want to. Brooks was optimistic, insisting that A.I.-enhanced robots would be allies, not threats.

Scientist-turned-author Clarke, on the other hand, was pessimistic. He told me intelligence will win out, and humans would likely compete for survival with super-intelligent machines. He wasn't specific about what would happen when we share the planet with super-intelligent machines, but he felt it'd be a struggle for mankind that we wouldn't win.

That went against everything I had thought about A.I., so I began interviewing artificial intelligence experts.

What evidence do you have to support your idea?
Advanced artificial intelligence is a dual-use technology, like nuclear fission, capable of great good or great harm. We're just starting to see the harm.

The NSA privacy scandal came about because the NSA developed very sophisticated data-mining tools. The agency used its power to plumb the metadata of millions of phone calls and the the entirety of the Internet—critically, all email. Seduced by the power of data-mining A.I., an agency entrusted to protect the Constitution instead abused it. They developed tools too powerful for them to use responsibly.

Today, another ethical battle is brewing about making fully autonomous killer drones and battlefield robots powered by advanced A.I.—human-killers without humans in the loop. It's brewing between the Department of Defense and the drone and robot makers who are paid by the DOD, and people who think it's foolhardy and immoral to create intelligent killing machines. Those in favor of autonomous drones and battlefield robots argue that they'll be more moral—that is, less emotional, will target better and be more disciplined than human operators. Those against taking humans out of the loop are looking at drones' miserable history of killing civilians, and involvement in extralegal assassinations. Who shoulders the moral culpability when a robot kills? The robot makers, the robot users, or no one? Nevermind the technical hurdles of telling friend from foe.

In the longer term, as experts in my book argue, A.I. approaching human-level intelligence won't be easily controlled; unfortunately, super-intelligence doesn't imply benevolence. As A.I. theorist Eliezer Yudkowsky of MIRI [the Machine Intelligence Research Institute] puts it, "The A.I. does not love you, nor does it hate you, but you are made of atoms it can use for something else." If ethics can't be built into a machine, then we'll be creating super-intelligent psychopaths, creatures without moral compasses, and we won't be their masters for long.

What is new about your thinking?
Individuals and groups as diverse as American computer scientist Bill Joy and MIRI have long warned that we have much to fear from machines whose intelligence eclipses our own. In *Our Final Invention*, I argue that A.I. will also be misused on the development path to human-level intelligence. Between today and the day when scientists create human-level intelligence, we'll have A.I.-related mistakes and criminal applications.

Why hasn't more been done, or, what is being done to stop AI from turning on us?
There's not one reason, but many. Some experts don't believe we're close enough to creating human-level artificial intelligence and beyond to worry about its risks. Many A.I. makers win contracts with the Defense Advanced Research Projects Agency [DARPA] and don't want to raise issues they consider political. The normalcy bias is a cognitive bias that prevents people from reacting to disasters and disasters in the making—that's definitely part of it. But a lot of A.I. makers are doing something. Check out the scientists who advise MIRI. And, a lot more will get involved once the dangers of advanced A.I. enter mainstream dialogue.

Can you describe a moment when you knew this was big?
We humans steer the future not because we're the fastest or the strongest creatures on the planet, but because we're the smartest.

When we share the planet with creatures smarter than ourselves, they'll steer the future. When I understood this idea, I felt I was writing about the most important question of our time.

Every big thinker has predecessors whose work was crucial to his discovery. Who gave you the foundation to build your idea?
The foundations of A.I. risk analysis were developed by mathematician I. J. Good, science fiction writer Vernor Vinge, and others including A.I. developer Steve Omohundro. Today, MIRI and Oxford's Future of Humanity Institute are almost alone in addressing this problem. *Our Final Invention* has about 30 pages of endnotes acknowledging these thinkers.

In researching and developing your idea, what has been the high point? And the low point?
The high points were writing *Our Final Invention,* and my ongoing dialogue with A.I. makers and theorists. People who program A.I. are aware of the safety issues and want to help come up with safeguards. For instance, MIRI is working on creating "friendly" A.I.

Computer scientist and theorist Steve Omohundro has advocated a "scaffolding" approach, in which provably safe A.I. helps build the next generation of A.I. to ensure that it too is safe. Then that A.I. does the same, and so on. I think a public-private partnership has to be created to bring A.I.-makers together to share ideas about security—something like the International Atomic Energy Agency, but in partnership with corporations. The low points? Realizing that the best, most advanced A.I. technology will be used to create weapons. And those weapons eventually will turn against us.

What two or three people are most likely to try to refute your argument? Why?
Inventor Ray Kurzweil is the chief apologist for advanced technologies. In my two interviews with him, he claimed that

we would meld with the A.I. technologies through cognitive enhancements. Kurzweil and people broadly called transhumanists and singularitarians think A.I. and ultimately artificial general intelligence and beyond will evolve with us. For instance, computer implants will enhance our brains' speed and overall capabilities. Eventually, we'll develop the technology to transport our intelligence and consciousness into computers. Then super-intelligence will be at least partly human, which in theory would ensure super-intelligence was "safe."

For many reasons, I'm not a fan of this point of view. Trouble is, we humans aren't reliably safe, and it seems unlikely that super-intelligent humans will be either. We have no idea what happens to a human's ethics after their intelligence is boosted. We have a biological basis for aggression that machines lack. Super-intelligence could very well be an aggression multiplier.

Who will be most affected by this idea?
Everyone on the planet has much to fear from the unregulated development of super-intelligent machines. An intelligence race is going on right now. Achieving A.G.I. is job number one for Google, IBM and many smaller companies like Vicarious and Deep Thought, as well as DARPA, the NSA and governments and companies abroad. Profit is the main motivation for that race. Imagine one likely goal: a virtual human brain at the price of a computer. It would be the most lucrative commodity in history. Imagine banks of thousands of PhD quality brains working 24/7 on pharmaceutical development, cancer research, weapons development and much more. Who wouldn't want to buy that technology?

Meanwhile, 56 nations are developing battlefield robots, and the drive is to make them, and drones, autonomous. They will be machines that kill, unsupervised by humans. Impoverished nations will be hurt most by autonomous drones and battlefield robots. Initially, only rich countries will be able to afford autonomous kill bots, so rich nations will wield these weapons against human soldiers from impoverished nations.

How might it change life, as we know it?

Imagine: in as little as a decade, a half-dozen companies and nations field computers that rival or surpass human intelligence. Imagine what happens when those computers become expert at programming smart computers. Soon we'll be sharing the planet with machines thousands or millions of times more intelligent than we are. And, all the while, each generation of this technology will be weaponized. Unregulated, it will be catastrophic.

What questions are left unanswered?

Solutions. The obvious solution would be to give the machines a moral sense that makes them value human life and property. But programming ethics into a machine turns out to be extremely hard. Moral norms differ from culture to culture, they change over time, and they're contextual. If we humans can't agree on when life begins, how can we tell a machine to protect life? Do we really want to be safe, or do we really want to be free? We can debate it all day and not reach a consensus, so how can we possibly program it?

We also, as I mentioned earlier, need to get A.I. developers together. In the 1970s, recombinant DNA researchers decided to suspend research and get together for a conference at Asilomar in Pacific Grove, California. They developed basic safety protocols like "don't track the DNA out on your shoes," for fear of contaminating the environment with genetic works in progress. Because of the "Asilomar Guidelines," the world benefits from genetically modified crops, and gene therapy looks promising. So far as we know, accidents were avoided. It's time for an Asilomar Conference for A.I.

What's standing in the way?

A huge economic wind propels the development of advanced A.I. Human-level intelligence at the price of a computer will be the hottest commodity in history. Google and IBM won't want to share their secrets with the public or competitors. The Department of Defense won't want to open their labs to China and Israel, and vice-versa. Public awareness has to push policy towards openness and public-private partnerships designed to ensure safety.

What is next for you?

I'm a documentary filmmaker, so of course I'm thinking about a film version of *Our Final Invention.*

"If we end up in Hell rather than Heaven, this time it will be our own fault. Regardless, there's no need to panic quite yet."

Experts Say AI Unlikely to Be an Existential Threat

Sidney Perkowitz

In this viewpoint, Sidney Perkowitz explores the central AI question: will it enhance our lives, usher in our decline, or something in between. To find answers, he contrasts two recent books by AI experts Murray Shanahan and John Markoff. While these writers differ in approach and conclusions, they agree that the threat of self-improving machines running amok is slim. Nonetheless, both are concerned with the dangerous implications of increasingly powerful AI now. Each writer balances the doomsday AI scenario with enough history and context to suggest that human agency can remain part of the equation as AI develops. Sidney Perkowitz is the author of Digital People *and other books and articles about science and technology.*

This essay, "Removing Humans from the AI Loop — Should We Panic?" by Sidney Perkowitz, was first published at the Los Angeles Review of Books on February 18, 2016. Reprinted by permission.

As you read, consider the following questions:

1. By what technical process does Murray Shanahan think we can engineer AI?
2. What theoretical paradox emerged from the AI research of the 1960s?
3. How does AI differ from "intelligence augmentation"?

If you think the main existential threat facing humanity is climate change or global food shortages, think again. A number of eminent scientists and technologists believe a bigger threat is the rise of powerful artificial intelligences (AI). They argue that these intelligences will dominate or replace humanity. "We are summoning the demon," Elon Musk, founder of Tesla Motors and SpaceX, recently said. "We should be very careful about artificial intelligence. If I were to guess, like, what our biggest existential threat is, it's probably that." Bill Gates shares these concerns, and Stephen Hawking put it apocalyptically when he told the BBC, "the development of full artificial intelligence could spell the end of the human race."

Others profoundly disagree. Eric Horvitz, who directs Microsoft's Redmond Research Lab—heavily involved in AI— thinks losing control of the technology "isn't going to happen." According to him, "we'll be able to get incredible benefits from machine intelligence in all realms of life, from science to education to economics to daily life."

Of course, countless science fiction works have portrayed imagined machine beings, such as HAL in Stanley Kubrick's *2001*. The classic film *Colossus: The Forbin Project* (1970) portrays an AI running amok and ruling humanity. The conceit has obviously become a popular generator of fictional plots. But Musk and the others are talking about the real world, our world. The pressing question becomes: Should we panic?

Or should we just accept defeat and hope our machine overlords won't be too brutal? Or, in a more hopeful mood, look to a golden age mediated by kindly superintelligences? Or, in a more indifferent one, file all these comments under "techno overhype" and go about our business?

Several recent books offer answers of a sort by examining the rise of the machine mind. Author of *The Technological Singularity*, Murray Shanahan is a professor at Imperial College London, where he conducts research on AI and robotics. Steeped since childhood in science fiction, he sees the value of the genre in presenting novel ideas—in the manner, for instance, of last year's robot film *Ex Machina*, for which he was a scientific advisor. His new book explores scenarios about the future of AI in somewhat similar fashion.

AI, he explains, can lead to a "technological singularity," a critical moment for humanity popularized by the futurist Ray Kurzweil, among others, who predicted it would arrive by the mid-21st century. The first person to call this event a "singularity" was the distinguished 20th-century mathematician John von Neumann, who thought breakneck technological progress would take us to "some essential singularity in the history of the race beyond which human affairs, as we know them, could not continue."

This may read like science fiction, but Shanahan points out that the idea is potentially meaningful for AI because AI is inherently dangerous. It can produce an unpredictable feedback loop: "When the thing being engineered is intelligence itself, the very thing doing the engineering, it can set to work improving itself. Before long, according to the singularity hypothesis, the ordinary human is removed from the loop."

Shanahan's tour of AI begins with the famous Turing test, developed from a seminal paper in 1950 by the British mathematician and World War II codebreaker Alan Turing. He predicted that machines would one day think well enough that a human interlocutor could not distinguish between a person and a machine. The "Turing test" criterion has yet to be met, but Shanahan suggests it's only a matter of time; in fact, he sketches out exactly how to build AIs possessing this and other "general intelligence" abilities.

One route to AI, "whole brain emulation," Shanahan explains, depends on the proposition that "human behavior is determined by physical processes in the brain." There are "no causal mysteries, no missing links, in the (immensely complicated) chain of causes and effects that leads from what we see, hear, and touch to what we do and say." In a human brain, the chain is built within 80 billion connected neurons, each taking nerve impulses as input and producing other impulses as output, which in turn activate other neurons. Shanahan's position is that we can build a brain by replicating those neurons with digital electronic elements in silicon chips. Some of us might object that what goes on in a human brain is more than what we see externally in a person's behavior. After all, we absolutely do not understand how and why neurons firing in the brain produce our individual internal realities: our sense of self or "consciousness." But setting aside that pesky issue, it is scientifically valid to propose that intelligence as manifested by behavior can be replicated by copying the brain behind the behavior.

Shanahan argues that the obstacles to building such a brain are technological, not conceptual. A whole human brain is more than we can yet copy, but we can copy one a thousand times smaller. That is, we are on our way, because existing digital technology could simulate the 70 million neurons in a mouse brain. If we can also map these neurons, then, according to Shanahan, it is only a matter of time before we can obtain a complete blueprint for an artificial mouse brain. Once that brain is built, Shanahan believes it would "kick-start progress toward human-level AI." We'd need to simulate billions of neurons of course, and then qualitatively "improve" the mouse brain with refinements like modules for language, but Shanahan thinks we can do both through better technology that deals with billions of digital elements and our rapidly advancing understanding of the workings of human cognition. To be sure, he recognizes that this argument relies on unspecified future breakthroughs.

But if we do manage to construct human-level AIs, Shanahan believes they would "almost inevitably" produce a next stage— namely, superintelligence—in part because an AI has big advantages over its biological counterpart. With no need to eat and sleep, it can operate nonstop; and, with its impulses transmitted electronically in nanoseconds rather than electrochemically in milliseconds, it can operate ultra-rapidly. Add the ability to expand and reproduce itself in silicon, and you have the seed of a scarily potent superintelligence.

Naturally, this raises fears of artificial masterminds generating a disruptive singularity. According to Shanahan, such fears are valid because we do not know how superintelligences would behave: "whether they will be friendly or hostile [...] predictable or inscrutable [...] whether conscious, capable of empathy or suffering." This will depend on how they are constructed and the "reward function" that motivates them. Shanahan concedes that the chances of AIs turning monstrous are slim, but, because the stakes are so high, he believes we must consider the possibility.

The singularity also appears in journalist John Markoff's *Machines of Loving Grace* (the title is from a Richard Brautigan poem), but only as a small part of a larger narrative about AI. John Markoff has written about technology, science, and computing for *The New York Times* since 1988, covering IBM-style mainframes to today's breakthroughs. From his base in San Francisco, he is well connected to Silicon Valley, and *Machines of Loving Grace* draws on Markoff's intimate knowledge of the research and researchers that form the AI enterprise. He begins with early AI work in the 1960s, which did not yield immediate success despite overly optimistic predictions. Same story in the 1980s. Signs of progress finally appeared around 1999, in products with rudimentary intelligence like Roomba, a vacuum cleaner that navigated itself around a house to suck up dirt; and Sony's Aibo, a mechanically cute robot dog that also autonomously navigated and responded to voice commands. Though not as smart as a two-year-old toddler or even a real dog, these devices possessed a sliver of general intelligence insofar as they could adapt to their environments in real time.

Early AI pioneers had differing notions of the relationship between intelligent machines and people. The Stanford computer scientist John McCarthy, who had coined the phrase "artificial intelligence," believed he could artificially emulate all human abilities (and do so within a decade). In contrast, Douglas Engelbart, a visionary engineer who had invented the computer mouse, worked on intelligent machines that would enhance human abilities to address the world's problems—an approach he called IA, "intelligence augmentation." In other words, as Markoff puts it: "One researcher attempted to replace human beings with intelligent machines [...] the other aimed to extend human capabilities." "Their work," he therefore argues, "defined both a dichotomy and a paradox." The paradox is that "the same technologies that extend the intellectual power of humans can displace them as well."

In the last decade, Markoff reports, AI research has produced commercial products that display both human extension and human displacement. One of them is speech recognition, which you encounter whenever you call your bank to get an account balance, or ask a question of Siri or Alexa, the personal assistants from Apple and Amazon, respectively. This will be important in satisfying the Turing test, and Siri and Alexa are examples of IA helping people manage their lives. On the other hand, Google's self-driving car, which can more or less safely navigate complex environments, eliminates the human driver.

These are not full human-level AIs—nor potential rogue superintelligences. They are merely steps in that direction.

Even if a singularity never actually happens, AI is already having serious social and economic effects. Markoff points out that robots have been taking over industrial jobs on auto assembly lines and elsewhere for decades. Now, with practicable AI, "workplace automation has started to strike the white-collar workforce with the same ferocity that it transformed the factory floor." Professionals such as doctors and airline pilots are not immune either.

But the option of IA, enhancement rather than replacement, makes it less likely that digital intelligences will dominate. Faith in pure AI does not come easily; when Markoff rides in a self-driving auto at 60 miles per hour, he finds it nerve-racking to "trust the car." People would likely get over this fear, but Markoff also notes that some surprisingly intricate situations can arise. At a four-way stop sign, drivers typically glance at each other to make sure each is following the rule "first in, first out." With self-driving cars, separate AIs would have to coordinate their actions, adding a hugely complicating layer of intercommunication technology to the process. Maybe the better answer is to keep people in the driver's seat, supported by IA in the form of smart sensors and software that make it easier and safer to drive.

In other applications, replacing people by synthetic versions might seem inhumane. With rising numbers of the elderly in the United States and Europe and a shortage of caregivers, some observers propose using robots instead. But would anyone want to be tended by machines? They might look human and display intelligence along with seeming compassion and "loving grace," but could they feel the "real" emotions that people want from truly involved caregivers? Calling the prospect "disturbing," Markoff suggests that we instead use IA to extend our ability to provide medical care, companionship, and better quality of life to the ill and elderly in human, person-to-person ways.

Taken together, the two books provide an overview of AI. They raise more questions than they answer, but that is to be expected. Both authors explain technical material lucidly with relatable examples. Their coverage sometimes overlaps, but their books are different. Shanahan's book is a compact (272 pages in a small format) science-based summary of the background and state of the AI art, with enough detail for the reader to grasp what is feasible, now and maybe later. At 400 pages, Markoff's book has less scientific detail but adds a rich story about the roots of AI and the people behind it, and its place in our daily world.

But back to the original question: Will AI lead to either an existential threat or an earthly paradise? Should we panic? While Markoff mentions the AI singularity, he is really interested in the less shattering effects AI has already had. Shanahan tells us how superintelligence might develop, but gives little reason to think this will happen in our lifetime.

For now, we are in charge of our machines. Shanahan tells us "we must decide what to do with the technology"; Markoff reminds us that the discussion of AI vs. IA is really about the "kind of world we will create."

If we end up in Hell rather than Heaven, this time it will be our own fault. Regardless, there's no need to panic quite yet.

"Technology has always been a double-edged sword, since fire kept us warm but also burned down our villages."

AI Will Benefit Humanity, Not Destroy It

Ray Kurzweil

In the following viewpoint, we'll hear from Ray Kurzweil, perhaps the most famous theorist and proponent of the singularity and a leading practitioner of AI research. Kurzweil dismisses technophobia as vastly overblown. In his view, all technology has potentially destructive side effects, if used irresponsibly. However, these should not prevent humanity from reaping the enormous benefit that increasing computing power and emerging AI will bring. Kurzweil points to other policies that have kept potentially dangerous technology in check and predicts we will have safe, human-level AI in less than two decades. Raymond "Ray" Kurzweil is an American author, computer scientist, inventor, and futurist.

"Don't Fear Artificial Intelligence," Ray Kurzweil, Kurzweil Accelerating Intelligence, December 30, 2014. Reprinted by permission.

As you read, consider the following questions:

1. Why is the author skeptical about apocalyptic fears regarding AI?
2. What reasons does Ray Kurzweil provide to back his optimism about technology?
3. How could AI technology be kept safe and benefit humans, according to this article?

S tephen Hawking, the pre-eminent physicist, recently warned that artificial intelligence (AI), once it surpasses human intelligence, could pose a threat to the existence of human civilization.

Elon Musk, the pioneer of digital money, private spaceflight and electric cars, has voiced similar concerns.

If AI becomes an existential threat, it won't be the first one. Humanity was introduced to existential risk when I was a child sitting under my desk during the civil defense drills of the 1950s.

Since then we have encountered comparable specters, like the possibility of a bioterrorist creating a new virus for which humankind has no defense. Technology has always been a double edged sword, since fire kept us warm but also burned down our villages.

The typical dystopian futurist movie has one or two individuals or groups fighting for control of "the AI." Or we see the AI battling the humans for world domination. But this is not how AI is being integrated into the world today. AI is not in one or two hands, it's in 1 billion or 2 billion hands.

A kid in Africa with a smartphone has more intelligent access to knowledge than the President of the United States had 20 years ago. As AI continues to get smarter, its use will only grow. Virtually everyone's mental capabilities will be enhanced by it within a decade.

We will still have conflicts among groups of people, each enhanced by AI. That is already the case. But we can take some comfort from a profound, exponential decrease in violence, as documented in Steven Pinker's 2011 book, *The Better Angels of Our Nature: Why Violence Has Declined.* According to Pinker, although the statistics vary somewhat from location to location, the rate of death in war is down hundredsfold compared with six centuries ago.

Since that time, murders have declined tensfold. People are surprised by this. The impression that violence is on the rise results from another trend: exponentially better information about what is wrong with the world—another development aided by AI.

There are strategies we can deploy to keep emerging technologies like AI safe. Consider biotechnology, which is perhaps a couple of decades ahead of AI. A meeting called the Asilomar Conference on Recombinant DNA was organized in 1975 to assess its potential dangers and devise a strategy to keep the field safe.

The resulting guidelines, which have been revised by the industry since then, have worked very well: there have been no significant problems, accidental or intentional, for the past 39 years. We are now seeing major advances in medical treatments reaching clinical practice and thus far none of the anticipated problems.

Consideration of ethical guidelines for AI goes back to Isaac Asimov's Three Laws of Robotics, which appeared in his short story "Runaround" in 1942, eight years before Alan Turing introduced the field of AI in his 1950 paper "Computing Machinery and Intelligence."

The median view of AI practitioners today is that we are still several decades from achieving human level AI. I am more optimistic and put the date at 2029, but either way, we do have time to devise ethical standards.

There are efforts at universities and companies to develop AI safety strategies and guidelines, some of which are already in place. Similar to the Asilomar guidelines, one idea is to clearly define the mission of each AI program and to build in encrypted safeguards to prevent unauthorized uses.

Ultimately, the most important approach we can take to keep AI safe is to work on our human governance and social institutions. We are already a human machine civilization.

The best way to avoid destructive conflict in the future is to continue the advance of our social ideals, which has already greatly reduced violence.

AI today is advancing the diagnosis of disease, finding cures, developing renewable clean energy, helping to clean up the environment, providing high quality education to people all over the world, helping the disabled—including providing Hawking's voice—and contributing in a myriad of other ways.

We have the opportunity in the decades ahead to make major strides in addressing the grand challenges of humanity. AI will be the pivotal technology in achieving this progress. We have a moral imperative to realize this promise while controlling the peril. It won't be the first time we've succeeded in doing this.

| "From democracy to cognition to social interactions, every social foundation will be renewed."

The Technological Singularity Will Force Us to Reorganize Our Values

Rodhlann Jornod

In the following viewpoint, Rodhlann Jornod suggests that we consider the technological singularity not as something to fear but as something we should control to create the society that we want. Since technology has always driven society and politics, there is no reason to believe the impending singularity—considered by many to be the fourth industrial revolution—will be any different. Jornod argues that we should make the effort now to predict the coming changes so that we can adapt positively. Rodhlann Jornod earned a Ph.D. at the Institute of Criminology in Paris, where he studied the structures of morality as related to criminal justice.

"At the Dawn of Political Upheaval Called the Singularity," Rodhlann Jornod, MyScienceWork, June 11, 2013. https://www.mysciencework.com/omniscience/at-the -dawn-of-political-upheaval-called-the-singularity. Licensed under CC BY-SA 3.0.

As you read, consider the following questions:

1. According to the author, theories about the technological singularity tend to come from what approach?
2. How does the author say human relationships are already changing?
3. What larger effect could technology like the 3D printer have?

I t seems risky not to question the ideology driving the changes foreseen by the technological singularity. It seems even more reckless not to try to predict the social impact of the acceleration of scientific progress. Our society is on the threshold of an era of tremendous political transformations that will be encouraged by technological progress. History will surely show us, once again, that technology determines politics.

Ideology vs. ideology

The real problem that the technological singularity will raise will be in the repercussions that the growth in knowledge will have on social transformations. Basically, which ideology will lead the technological revolution? The nootropics-boosted, exocortex-enhanced and dimensionally extended augmented man may be attainable, but which way will he lean politically?

For the most part, the theories structuring the concept of the technological singularity are fraught with liberalism. English-speaking thinkers took the risk of objectively confronting this notion, and most of the writings on the subject come from these researchers. Transhumanism made the technological singularity its own concept, and this theoretical current is not politically neutral. It oscillates between one kind of liberalism and another, that is, from social democracy to right-libertarianism. A thinker such as Kurzweil illustrates this perfectly. As a defender of both transhumanism and libertarianism, he participated in the development of the Singularity University with Google. This institution, which aims to grasp, in an interdisciplinary fashion, the impact of technological acceleration on humanity, exemplifies the fact that European research is lagging on this front. If the ideology of the Anglosphere gains control over this issue, the great risk could be its strongly utilitarian tinge. Utilitarianism becomes dangerous when the human being, as an individual, appears as a hindrance to humanity. Asimov's zeroth law tackles this issue and puts the interests of humanity before the interests of the human being.

A utilitarian and liberal programming of artificial intelligence could represent a real danger for living beings, which the machine could consider useless. However, as Slavoj Zizek says, it is easier to imagine the end of the world than a modest alteration of the political model. Liberalism has become the reality that will outlast humans.

Steering reflection from productivism to eudemonia could be a starting point to a revolution of the ideological approach to technology—some economists have made this choice when emphasizing gross national happiness over gross domestic product.

The singularity has to be approached with an awareness of the ideologies underlying the question of progress. The social struggles and the conflicts of interest that exist in the scientific and industrial fields have to enter the debate so that we can envision a technological growth focused on happiness—a sort of transhuman eudemonia.

From a utilitarian artificial intelligence emerges a friendly artificial intelligence, according to the results of Eliezer Yudkowsky's research. This could correspond to a political humanization of the artificial.

The preludes of a collective intelligence

From democracy to cognition to social interactions, every social foundation will be renewed. Relationships between humans are already being redesigned by social networks, which outline what appears to be a collective intelligence. The individuals' interconnection creates a network that gives shape to society's reactivity to an event. A collective empathy becomes more and more visible as the diffusion of information accelerates, thanks to tools like Twitter. This interconnection could be represented as a web on which every vibration rapidly spreads to the whole structure. The fact that tools like Wikipedia are within easy reach makes it possible to externalize memory, to free intelligence from the task of remembering, and give it the opportunity to evolve, as Michel Serres, in particular, claims. Collective intelligence is still in a passive state, with simple reaction providing satisfaction. This level, which could be qualified as emotional, is slowly giving way to an active rationality using socially distributed cognition.

In the political sphere, software programs have been able to create new models, notably with the concept of liquid democracy, which gathers the forces of direct and representative democracy. From technological creation emerges political creation. In the economic sphere, crowdfunding decentralizes fundraising by eliminating traditional intermediaries that slow down innovation. Technological advances allow individuals to regain the means of production and profoundly alter the contemporary economy. Between phenomena like the free culture movement, with the renewal of intellectual property rights, and the creation of devices, like the 3D printer, which give one the opportunity to take charge of the means of production, abandoned until now to industry, a major destabilization of the economic, industrial and liberal model promises to appear in the years to come.

There are not many choices:

1) The economic model could question its fundamental values and evolve. (Libertarianism is attempting this, particularly when it comes to intellectual property.)

2) A new economic model could emerge. The idea of the post-scarcity economy is being taken over by a notion of horizontality where the individual's interactions with his/her environment become more and more frequent.

3) The current model could try to make sure that the interests of a few people prevail over the common interests by

imposing more restrictions. We can observe this tendency with digital rights management in the face of an emerging diffusion of digital culture.

The interconnection of individuals that computer networks already augur opens up the possibility of the society of the global brain, where all beings will be linked like a nervous system that will act as a whole. The noosphere, introduced by the French philosopher Pierre Teilhard de Chardin, is the idea that the phenomenon of cognition is mutualized in a collective consciousness of humanity. It turns out that the concept foretold the technological revolution now underway. The outline of a cybernetic society starts to surface in this electronic swarming. This society's interactions will make it possible to self-regulate the interconnected entities and will constitute the very identity of a transcended humanity.

The environmental issue

The acceleration of the technological growth will raise another political question: transhuman ecology. The numerous environmental issues caused by the modern production model could increase with the technological progress of our time—with increasing space pollution, for instance. Waste management would then become a crucial issue related to scientific advances. A stance such as technogaianism considers technological progress not a threat, but rather a way to restore Earth's ecosystem. This idea is encouraged by scientific discoveries like nuclear fusion or artificial photosynthesis. The environmental perspectives are eminently of an ideological nature, whether we choose an anthropocentric approach or respect for the biosphere predominates. This opposition can be perceived as part of the deep ecology philosophy, which no longer gives priority to human interests, as traditional ecology does, in order to place them in the larger context of the interests of living things. Exploiting raw materials existing in space, for example through asteroid capture, especially for mining purposes, promises solutions to the overexploitation of Earth's resources. Even the eminent Stephen Hawking lends credibility to such science fiction dreams with his prediction that humanity's future resides in colonizing space.

The demographic explosion

Another fundamental ideological issue that the technological singularity raises concerns demographics. An acceleration of the medical discoveries, like the regeneration of organs using stem cells or even organ printing, could considerably increase life expectancy. Researchers even predict the quasi-immortality of the human being: even if longevity is only a few centuries long, the mind could be transferred in an android that would replace the body. Demographics have always encouraged social transformations throughout history. The demographic explosion that could happen along with the increase in longevity will inevitably transform humanity. Aubrey de Grey speaks of Methuselarity to describe a period when death would only come by accident or homicide. Humans would become Methuselahs in the making. There could be many outcomes of such population growth: wars between declining and growing populations—which could correspond to differences in access to healthcare—or some kind of gerontocracy, or even the development of space research to colonize neighboring planets (Mars One).

A time is coming where knowledge will bring knowledge, where the augmentation of humans will lead them to a reorganization of their values, and where science will assert itself as the driving force for social and political expansion. In this time, the necessity of reflection will be essential, in the hope of directing this future explosion of knowledge toward the greater good.

Periodical and Internet Sources Bibliography

The following articles have been selected to supplement the diverse views presented in this chapter.

Charles Arthur, "Artificial Intelligence: 'Homo sapiens will be split into a handful of gods and the rest of us,'" *Guardian*, November 7, 2015.

Mark Bishop, "Fear Artificial Stupidity, Not Artificial Intelligence," *New Scientist*, December 18, 2014.

Paul Ford, "Our Fear of Artificial Intelligence," *MIT Technology Review*, February 11, 2015.

Tia Ghose, "Intelligent Robots Will Overtake Humans by 2100, Experts Say," Live Science, May 7, 2013.

Jason Kashdan, "Is Artificial Intelligence Threat Looming?" CBS News, March 9, 2015.

Christof Koch, "Will Artificial Intelligence Surpass Our Own?" *Scientific American*, September 1, 2015.

Elizabeth Lee, "Scientists Warn AI Can Be Dangerous as Well as Helpful to Humans," Voice of America, May 11, 2016.

Nick Statt, "Bill Gates Is Worried About Artificial Intelligence Too," CNET, January 28, 2015.

For Further Discussion

Chapter 1

1. What do you see as the greatest obstacle to building a machine possessing general AI? Is this a philosophical concern about the nature of human experience, or a technical question about how we could build the machine? Explain your position.
2. Assuming for a moment that human-level machine intelligence is possible, would this be a good or bad thing for society?
3. How do current economic systems, politics, and other ideological constructs influence how we understand the role machine intelligence may have in the future?

Chapter 2

1. Do you think AI would free humanity to be more creative and productive? Or do you see more inequality and unemployment as likely results of further automation? Explain your answer.
2. Consumer capitalism and Silicon Valley tech companies are current drivers of narrow AI technology. Is this a good thing? Should more regulation and oversight be put in place to encourage better uses of this technology? Or should the market decide?
3. Increasing military uses of AI technology raises ethical concerns about future warfare. Do you think that it is better for battles to be fought by robot proxies than young citizens? What dangers might this precedent introduce?

Chapter 3

1. Do you believe the human being is an appropriate benchmark for AI? Do you think it is possible to create machine intelligence without using humans as a template?

2. Some observers have spoken of the need for emotionally intelligent machines. What types of intelligence should we encourage in our computer coding? Do computers always reflect the values of those who program them, or do you think a kind of universalism can be reached through impartial machine intelligence?

3. Do you think AI should have the same rights as humans? What ethical problems do you foresee from not granting them the same rights? What societal problems do you foresee if they are not granted the same rights?

Chapter 4

1. What are your feelings about the so-called super-intelligence explosion or Singularity? Does this seem likely?

2. If you allow for a possible future of Singularity, is this an existential threat to humans? Or do you think machines and humans can coexist peacefully?

3. Do you think machines can ever truly be self-aware or conscious? Does this matter?

Organizations to Contact

The editors have compiled the following list of organizations concerned with the issues debated in this book. The descriptions are derived from materials provided by the organizations. All have publications or information available for interested readers. The list was compiled on the date of publication of the present volume; the information provided here may change. Be aware that many organizations take several weeks or longer to respond to inquiries, so allow as much time as possible.

Allen Institute for Artificial Intelligence
(206) 548-5600
website: http://allenai.org

AI2 was founded in 2014 with the singular focus of conducting high-impact research and engineering in the field of artificial intelligence, all for the common good.

Association for the Advancement of Artificial (AAAI) Intelligence
2275 East Bayshore Road, Suite 160
Palo Alto, CA 94303
(650) 328-3123
website: https://www.aaai.org

AAAI is a nonprofit scientific society devoted to advancing the scientific understanding of the mechanisms underlying thought and intelligent behavior and their embodiment in machines.

Canadian Artificial Intelligence Association
email: butz@cs.uregina.ca
website: https://www.caiac.ca

CAIAC promotes interest and activity in AI by conducting workshops and a fully refereed national conference every year. It also sponsors the journal *Computational Intelligence*.

Future of Life Institute
Cambridge, MA
website: http://futureoflife.org

The Future of Life Institute (FLI) is a volunteer-run research and outreach organization that works to mitigate existential risks facing humanity, particularly existential risk from advanced artificial intelligence (AI).

Machine Intelligence Research Institute
2030 Addison Street, Floor 7
Berkeley, CA 94704
website: https://intelligence.org

The Machine Intelligence Research Institute is a research nonprofit studying the mathematical underpinnings of intelligent behavior.

Open AI
website: https://openai.com/about

OpenAI is a nonprofit artificial intelligence research company. Its goal is to advance digital intelligence in the way that is most likely to benefit humanity as a whole, unconstrained by a need to generate financial return.

SRI International
333 Ravenswood Avenue
Menlo Park, CA 94025-3493
(650) 859-2000
website: https://www.sri.com/about/organization/information
-computing-sciences/aic

SRI's Artificial Intelligence Center (AIC) is one of the world's major centers of research in artificial intelligence (AI). Since its founding in 1966, the AIC has been pioneering and contributing to the development of computer capabilities for intelligent behavior in complex situations.

Bibliography of Books

James Barrat. *Our Final Invention: Artificial Intelligence and the End of the Human Era.* New York, NY: Thomas Dunne Books, 2013.

Anthony Berglas. *When Computers Can Think: The Artificial Intelligence Singularity.* CreateSpace, 2015.

Nick Bostrom. *Superintelligence.* Oxford, UK: Oxford University Press, 2014.

John Brockman. *What to Think About Machines That Think: Today's Leading Thinkers on the Age of Machine Intelligence.* New York, NY: Harper Perennial, 2015.

Calum Chace. *The Economic Singularity.* CreateSpace, 2016.

Louis A. Del Monte. *The Artificial Intelligence Revolution: Will Artificial Intelligence Serve Us or Replace Us?* Louis A. Del Monte, 2013.

Amnon H. Eden. *Singularity Hypothesis.* New York, NY: Springer, 2015.

Martin Ford. *Rise of the Robots.* New York, NY: Perseus Books, 2015.

Michael C. Harris. *Artificial Intelligence.* New York, NY: Marshall Cavendish Benchmark, 2011.

Kathryn Hulick. *Artificial Intelligence.* Minneapolis, MN: Essential Library, 2016.

P. Andrew Karam. *Artificial Intelligence.* New York, NY: Chelsea House, 2011.

Kevin Kelly. *The Inevitable.* New York, NY: Viking Press, 2016.

Ray Kurzweil. *How to Create a Mind.* New York, NY: Penguin, 2013.

Ray Kurzweil. *The Singularity Is Near*. New York, NY: Penguin, 2006.

James D. Miller. *Singularity Rising: Surviving and Thriving in a Smarter, Richer, and More Dangerous World*. Dallas, TX: Benbella Books, 2015.

Vincent C. Muller. *Risks of Artificial Intelligence*. Boca Raton, FL: CRC Press, 2016.

Q. L. Pearce. *Artificial Intelligence*. Detroit, MI: Lucent Books, 2011.

Stuart J. Russell, Peter Norvig, and Ernest Davis. *Artificial Intelligence: A Modern Approach*. Upper Saddle River, NJ: Prentice Hall, 2010.

Susan Schneider. *Science Fiction and Philosophy: From Time Travel to Superintelligence*. Hoboken, NJ: Wiley, 2016.

Murray Shanahan. *The Technological Singularity*. Cambridge, MA: MIT Press, 2015.

Roman V. Yampolskiy. *Artificial Superintelligence: A Futuristic Approach*. Boca Raton, FL: Taylor and Francis, CRC Press, 2016.

Index